Copyright © 2018 by Karl Moeller. All rights reserved.

'Among the Sleeping' previously published in
'Celebrating Divine Presence,' © Companion Books, 2009

'Succession' previously published in
'OmPoint Circular International', online publication, 2015
©OmPoint Productions

Cover, book design and layout by Karl Moeller
Font Bodoni SvtyTwo ITC

ISBN 978-0-692-06424-5

karl.moeller@me.com

AMB Publishing resides in the hearts of man

———————————

ALSO BY KARL MOELLER

Chapter in *Celebrating Divine Presence*
©Companion Books 2009

Contributor and Layoutwalla for
Beads On One String: Heartland Pilgrimage
©AMB Publishing 2013

Novel, *Return To Treasure Island*
©AMB Publishing 2014

**All titles are available on
amazon.com and barnes&noble.com**

AMONG THE SLEEPING:
SUFISM
Within and Without
ISLAM

KARL MOELLER

FOREWORD BY *Talat Halman, Ph.D*
Associate Professor of Religion

*"Out beyond ideas of
wrongdoing and rightdoing
there is a field.
I'll meet you there."*

Maulana Jelalludin Rumi

AUTHOR'S NOTE

Throughout America, the United Kingdom and Europe, anti-Islamist feelings are at an alarming level. In reality, murderous radicals justifying their acts using fine print in the Qur'an bear no more relation to Islam than the Ku Klux Klan does to Christianity. So-called Jihadists hide behind religion, but their motives are more prosaic - political, territorial and financial power.

Fear and ignorance, fueled by irresponsible journalism, have inflamed Western prejudices against Muslims. Anti-immigration sentiment is rampant. The irony is that mideastern refugees are fleeing various conflicts waged by the same 'Islamic' radicals many in the West fear so deeply.

Within the Muslim world, the Sufi Orders are a movement dedicated to the spiritual evolution of mankind, one 'murid' at a time. They are, within the Islamic world, a potent contrast to radical fundamentalist fighters.

This book is a nonacademic introduction and an attempt to describe Muslim spirituality, embodied by people in Sufi orders, historically and to the present day. It is an attempt to inform and educate those with a sincere interest in their own spiritual evolution.

Karl Moeller
2018

Knowing full well I have not
the wisdom for this task,
I undertake it and call upon
al-Razzaq, Allah The Sustainer.

The Kalimah

"La Ilaha Illah Allah wa
Muhammad ar-Rasul Allah"

"There is no god but God and
Muhammad is his Prophet"

FOREWORD

THIS SMALL BOOK ON SUFISM IS A MASTERPIECE. It surveys the vast range of types of Sufism as well as the vast ranges of phenomena and traditions -- both in Islamic Sufism and in Universalist Sufism. Karl Moeller clearly explains Sufism's roots in the Prophet Muhammad's mission and his teachings and practices. It includes sufficient information on the foundations of the Prophet's example and the Qur'an for the novice to proceed into this survey of Sufism. Passages from Qur'an and *hadith* have been deftly selected. He discusses the relationship of Sufism to Islam.

He explains the model of spiritual psychological transformation, the seven levels of the soul. The role of saints (Wali) and of Axial Saints (Qutb) is clarified. That chapter also explains the attributed spiritual blessing-power (baraka) that saints are sought out for. Moeller explains the practice of seeking intercession through saints. The very popular, wide-spread practice of visiting (*ziyara*) saints' tombs is discussed and described.

A beautiful feature of this book is the explanation of the dynamics of lineage and the samples of actual lineage-succession lists (*silsila*). The teacher-student or master disciple relationship, so central to Sufism, receives extensive analysis. Sufi meditational practices (*zikr*) and the spirituality of listening (*sema*) to sacred music are discussed. A great number of Sufi-lineage traditions (*tariqa*) are discussed in depth and others are listed.

Moeller also comprehensively surveys contemporary expressions of Sufism, both globally and in Europe and America. Delightfully, Moeller includes the Sufi wisdom-humor stories of Mulla Nasruddin Hoja. There is even a sort of "FAQ" included. Copious quotes from Sufis, including Rumi, appear.

H. TALAT HALMAN, Ph.D.

Associate Professor, Religion
Central Michigan University

AMONG THE SLEEPING
SUFISM WITHIN AND WITHOUT ISLAM

TABLE OF CONTENTS   PG.

INTRODUCTION..	1
QUESTIONS AND ANSWERS...........................	7
ISLAM AND THE PROPHET.............................	17
EARLY SUFIS...	25
SUFISM AND SHARIA.....................................	31
SUFI ORDERS..	39
THE TRUE TEACHER.....................................	47
TEACHING METHODS...................................	57
AMONG THE SLEEPING.................................	73
MORE QUESTIONS AND ANSWERS....................	77
SUFISM WITHOUT ISLAM..............................	83
SUFIS WITHOUT ORDER...............................	91
PRESENT-DAY MUSLIM SUFI ORDERS...............	95
SCI-FI SUFIS...	113
TIME, PLACE, AND PEOPLE..........................	115
IN CONCLUSION...	116
SUFISM AND JIHADISTS.................................	117
SUCCESSION: MURSHIDA RABIA MARTIN AND THE PASSING OF HAZRAT INAYAT KHAN......	129
MY STORY..	169
ARABIC/PERSIAN GLOSSARY..........................	177
BIBLIOGRAPHY..	185

Among the Sleeping

INTRODUCTION

"Any sufficiently advanced technology is indistinguishable from magic."

British science-fiction author Arthur C. Clarke wrote this in 1961. He was right. Recent scientific and lay writing on quantum physics utilizes terms such as multidimensionality, quarks, particle/wave duality, link theory, and Planck's constant. Close reading reveals that cutting-edge physics denies the existence of time and the reality of physical matter, the latter being a mere series of improbability curves. Physics may as well be magic. One would not expect a reader to instantly grasp what can take physicists a lifetime to master. However, over time, even an interested layman may, through repetition and multiple examples, get a mental glimpse of the unsuspected reality.

But the subject is Sufism. What is Sufism? It is a guided mystical path, a course of training, predicated on the concepts that mysticism is a science, and that spirituality can be systematically unveiled in those with the right potential for love. Sufism's 'classical' period was 1200 to 800 years ago, in a MidEast culture much different from the modern, postindustrial West, lived by Muslims speaking or writing in Arabic or medieval Persian or Turkish, describing human experiences quite alien to ours – it may as well be science fiction or quantum physics.

However, in all these efforts, we are trying to use words to describe something far more complex than quantum physics. Persons far advanced on the Path might argue that Sufism and quantum physics are one and the same, except that the Sufi ascribes infinite consciousness to the universe and its Creator, while the best the physicist can do is hold up an 'uncertainty principle.'

This book will present Islamic and Sufi concepts along with their original Arabic or Persian terms; just as a physicist finds it impossible to totally avoid his discipline's jargon, so must those interested in Sufism begin to learn the terms that practitioners actually employ. (See the 'Arabic/Persian Glossary' chapter.)

INCLUDED DISCUSSIONS

1. The Prophet Muhammad (570-632) and the history and spread of Islam.
2. Muhammad's own spiritual practices, which inspired the early Sufis.
3. Famous Sufi orders and their founders.
4. Sufi poetry and teaching-stories written over the past 1400 years, which attempt to describe the inner states of realization.
5. Apparent practitioner miracles.
6. How Sufism is based on and interrelates with Islam.

With the use of strained metaphors, teaching stories and quotations from 1400 years of Islam and Sufi tradition, the goal here is, like a pointillist painter, to create a recognizable outline of Islamic Sufism with at least a little detail right there in the middle. We are, in the end, simply confounded by our conditioning, lack of like experience, by the use of imperfectly translated words in a different language from the original practitioners, and by the ineffable quality that defines the Sufi.

Any discussion of Sufism is further complicated by the fact that words are themselves metaphors, mere stand-ins for the real thing or experience; the meaning derived from reading a sequence of words is utterly dependent upon the experience of the person reading them.

SURRENDER

If the term applies to those who systematically attempt to live so as to invite God into their beings, then Sufis state that there have always been Sufis. There are records going back centuries before Christ, indicating there were active groups of dedicated Zoroastrian mystics. The Essenes have been referred to as a mystic brotherhood. The Gnostic Gospels' Acts of John describe a Dervish-like dance at the Last Supper, with Jesus in the middle leading a call and response litany.

However, for over 1400 years, Sufism has been defined by and seen as an extension of traditional Islam; the terms and methods are inextricably Muslim. Islam is the exoteric religion. Sufism is mysticism, esoteric practice in an Islamic wrapper. "Islam" literally means 'surrender,' to the will of God, or Allah. In the West we tend to associate surrender with subservience, and have lost touch with its hidden power.

The only places in the West available to the public where surrender is ever discussed is in the process of substance abuse recovery, in the various 'Anonymous' groups. This is an interesting parallel, since advanced Sufis consider the bulk of mankind to be addicted to their hypnotized and spiritually asleep state. Similar to an AA group, the would-be Sufi also has to systematically surrender to the Higher Power, making amends, and 'recovering' from the 'sleep' state, gaining the inner sight of which some are capable.

Surrender creates an empty space within the psyche which allows us to experience the power of our true Self without being overwhelmed or inflated. Sufi practices are designed to help man to surrender, and to realize that man can become infinite, that we are not contained by the limited horizons of the mind and ego.

In the Sufi view, the practice of systematic surrender begins with an understanding of Islam, study of the Qur'an, and absorbing the ongoing impact of the life and example of the Prophet Muhammad.

QUESTIONS AND ANSWERS

WHAT IS SUFISM ?

Sufism is the Science of erasure of Self into the Creator, and alignment with His will. Sufism is also the Path of the Heart. Mankind is in a deep sleep or dream; Sufism consists of the individual waking to the true Reality and to our true divine nature.

WHAT DO SUFIS BELIEVE?

The Sufi Work has existed in every age of man. The Sufi Orders and their energies exist today. Communication between Sufis is possible without physical presence. A developed Sufi creates something permanent which continues after death. Therefore, the founders of each order can still be contacted directly, and visits to the tomb of a founder are often recommended. Practitioner miracles are a byproduct, not the goal, of higher consciousness.

ARE THERE SUFI PLACES IN THE WORLD?

Sufi organizations come into being for specific work and may dissolve when the work is completed. Sometimes the burial places of the founders of various orders — such as Abdul Qadir Gilani (1077-1166) in Baghdad, Iraq and Moinuddin Chishti (1141-1236) in Ajmer, India — have active groups nearby.

WHO WERE SOME SUFIS THAT WERE GENUINE?

Some Sufis are *mashhur*, or well known, and some are *mastur*, secret, or hidden. Many effective Sufis were/are hidden and are not teachers, and therefore unknown. Names — there are thousands, but the most prominent are those who were ordered to, or who willingly took on the teaching role, and thus were the nuclei of the Orders mentioned in this document, such as Abdul Qadir Gilani, Bahauddin Naqshband, Suhrawardi, Maulana Rumi, Moinuddin Chishti.

WHAT DOES 'GENUINE' MEAN?

It means participating in a living chain of personally transmitted knowledge and wisdom;

it means attracting *murids* with the ability and willingness to surrender, and an illumined murshid to effect the change. Because of these rigorous requirements it is possible to encounter, not an active, living order, but rather an ineffective remnant cult.

WHAT DOES SUFISM HAVE TO OFFER PEOPLE IN TODAY'S SOCIETY?

If you mean fast-paced, post-industrial Western culture where money is a religion, where the individual is redefined as a consumer, creature comforts are all important, and generations of television watching have conditioned people to expect a positive resolution of every dilemma within a half hour, then the regretful reply is 'not much.' People so deeply conditioned are not suitable subjects, too deeply 'asleep' for Sufism's course of study.

Real understanding and growth takes a lot of consideration and reflection, and requires unprecedented cooperation between the head and the heart, as well as an accomplished guide. No one can perceive the will of God alone.

Most human pursuits and characteristics may be defined in terms of a statistical bell curve – intelligence, empathy, strength, etc. A characteristic of any bell curve is that high functioning people are very much in the numeric minority, out there on the thin right end of the curve. If Sufism is considered an effective path to the final stage of human evolution, it requires remarkable subjects with real capabilities and paradoxically humble attitudes.

CAN SUFIS PERFORM MIRACLES?

Enough stories exist to indicate the answer is 'yes, on occasion,' or 'yes, of necessity.' There are two levels of paranormal experience occasionally encountered among Sufis. One is *firasat*, or intuitive insight, often cited in *murid-murshid* relations. The other is the outright miracle, *karamat*. However, the advanced Sufi would not consider either of these to be a miracle, but rather a necessary occurrence in accord with the wish and will of Allah. If the occurrence seems to violate laws of time and space, the Sufi would invite the observer to consider who created these so-called 'laws.'

ARE SUFIS LIBERAL, ORTHODOX, NEITHER?

As always, it depends upon context. In this world age, 'Eastern' Sufis – in or from their original countries – use terms and methods based on and interrelated with Islam, and may therefore be considered orthodox. As has been mentioned, many prominent Sufis of the classical era, such as al-Ghazzali and ibn-al-Arabi, were prominent jurists. However, relative to fundamentalist Muslims, most Sufi Orders are considered wildly liberal and unconventional.

THEN MUST SUFIS BE MUSLIMS?

The traditionalist, if that term may be applied to Sufism within Islam, answer is 'yes.' The following, fairly representative 'traditionalist' statement comes from Dr. Javad Nurbakhsh (1926-2008), Murshid of the Nimatullahi Order of Sufis in Tehran, Iran (Shia):

> "The term 'Sufism' has meaning only in the context of Islam. That is to say, outside Islam, Sufism does not exist – for it is the fruit of the tree of Islam. Although one might find traces of Sufism in other religions and philosophical schools,

these cannot be taken to be Sufism as a whole. The name 'sufi' is synonymous with a follower of 'Ali, himself the disciple (and spiritual successor) of the Prophet of Islam, Muhammad.

Since a Sufi must be a Moslem, to be a sufi while not fulfilling the duties and obligations of Islam is an impossibility. With this in mind, one can distinguish those self-centered and ambitious individuals who detach Sufism from Islam and set themselves up as 'sufi masters.' One should realize that removing Sufism from Islam will result only in a psuedo-Sufism, devoid of Sufism's true essence. Such a graft onto the tree of other philosophical schools or religions can result only in a dead branch. The living fruit of Sufism, however, grows only on the tree of Islam, and only a true Moslem can receive the fragrance of its blossoms.

Thus, whatever is not of Islam is not Sufism; and whoever is not a Moslem is not a Sufi."

Rumi seems to disagree, in this quatrain:

> Two hands, two feet, two eyes, good,
> As it should be, but no separation of the Friend and your loving.
> Any dividing there makes other untrue distinctions Like 'Jew' and 'Christian' and 'Muslim.'

The irony regarding this question is that, within the Muslim world, as discussed, there are fundamentalist groups who see all Sufi Orders as saint worshippers, using saints as intermediaries to God, and presenting undesirable innovations, *bid'aa* – to Islam.

THEN WHO MAY BE CONSIDERED A SUFI?

Suhrawardi, in his 'A Sufi Rule For Novices' (*muridin*), discusses the people described as *mutashabbihun*, or 'people who try to resemble Sufis.' Suhrawardi makes a convincing case that these people are truly associated with Sufism, and quotes two supporting *hadith*:

> "Whoever makes an effort to resemble a group of people is one of them."

"Man is associated with those whom he loves."

Suhrawardi stresses that even though these people emulating Sufis don't take on all the obligations incumbent upon initiates into an order, it is by their aspiration (*iradah*) that these people are one with the Sufis, similar to a regular novice, whose title *murid* means 'aspirant'.

One could properly say that the effectiveness of the teaching and transmission in any order, anywhere, will reflect in the inner qualities developed in its murids – are the results permanent, and do they result in detachment, or attachment? Only very long observation, or a developed Sufi, can tell if the changes are real, or simply acting or wishful thinking.

Answers to question about Sufism will vary according to the state of the questioner. The *murid*, or aspirant, will be concerned with the external aspect of Sufism, mutual relations or ethics. This is the exact place which the "Muslim vs. nonMuslim" Sufi question occupies. A Sufi of the middle rank, *mutawassit*, will be interested in the inner states, or *ahwal*, available to his abilities. The *arif*, or knower, will be conveyed a touch of *haqiqa*, Reality.

The beginning of Sufism is learning, the middle is practice, and the end is nothing less than Grace.

AMONG THE SLEEPING

ISLAM AND THE PROPHET

Within Islam, there are Five Pillars which are the framework of Muslim life: testimony of faith (*Kalimah*), prayer (*Salat*), concern for the needy (*Zakat*), self-purification (*Sawm, Ramadhan*), and *Hajj*, the pilgrimage to Mecca, for those who are able.

There are also clear guidelines of behavior for the Muslim believer, in order of severity of consequence after death. However, these all refer to external, observable behavior, which may or may not be accompanied by genuine personal change or even belief. One may scrupulously follow every one of these guidelines, while being motivated by nothing more exalted than a fear of Hell.

Muslims are expected to follow not just the words and actions of the Prophet Muhammad (the *Sunna*), but also to attempt to attain the states of his being, his states of the heart, such as god-fearingness (*taqwa*), mercy (*rahma*), reliance (*tawakkul*) upon Allah, humility, sincerity, and many others. Sufis believe these states are desirable, not because of fear of Hell, but because the Prophet Muhammad was *'insani kamil'* – the Completed Man, the best and most lovable of men, the most worthy of honor and emulation, and he carried the words and decrees of an irresistibly lovable God.

Exact instructions on how to achieve these surrendered states of the Prophet are not in the Qur'an, nor in books of Islamic jurisprudence, because unlike prayer, gifts to the poor, or fasting, there are no hard and fast guidelines, universally applicable, for each soul, no single recipe for enlightenment.

Hadith, the authenticated utterances of the Prophet, and many Qur'anic verses illustrate repeatedly that not only must a Muslim do and say certain things, but must also change internally, become something new, must clean his or her heart. These changes may only be acquired with considerable, right-minded effort, termed 'purification' in many places in the Qur'an.

"He has succeeded who purifies himself" (Qur'an 87.14).

But the Qur'an tells the Muslim only that change is obligatory; it does not say specifically how. This is where the example set and internal states experienced by the Prophet become crucial to understanding the methods and goals of Sufi training.

Systematically bringing about this change in the individual is the aim of the Islamic science of Sufism.

THE PROPHET'S EXAMPLE

The Prophet Muhammad is seen by all Eastern, traditional Sufi orders as the Gnosis of Reality, *marefat-e-haqiqat,* or the Complete Man, *insani kamil.* Born Muhammad ibn Abdullah ibn Abdul Muttalib ibn Hashim, he lived from 570 to 632. The Prophet and his close associates, the Companions, exceeded all requirements in regard to prayer and devotional practices. All through his life, he kept long night vigils and often practiced voluntary fasts. He never ate barley bread, which was a staple at that time, on three consecutive days, and he never ate wheat bread, which was considered a luxury. One of his favorite sayings was "Poverty is my pride," and this saying came to be quoted in every manual of Sufi doctrine, making the rule of poverty a basic characteristic, at least theoretically, of Sufi life.

Going back to antiquity, the prevalent model of a mystic is one with a quiet, modest, retiring demeanor, vegetarian, dressed implausibly, head in the clouds, impractical, residing in a monastery or a cave, in order to eliminate distractions and temptations from the noisome outer world. History does indeed show various Sufi monasteries around the Mideast and East. But a quatrain from the Sufi poet Hafiz (1310-1325) tells us:

> Come to the tavern
> Drink the wine
> Go not to the cell-squatters in the monastery
> For their deeds are dark.

The Prophet did, at age 40, spend time in meditation in a cave near Mecca, ending with a visit from the Angel Gabriel (Jibreel in Arabic), who said, "Rise, for thou art the Prophet of God. Go forth and preach in the name of thy Lord. Your God is merciful." After this mystical experience, Muhammad left the cave – but he was visited by Jibreel many times in the next 23 years.

The Prophet Muhammad was an orphan, then a successful trader, husband, father, widower, legislator, educator, warrior, and general. The Sufi, whether in the East or West, may be involved in literally any profession, meeting his or her societal and familial obligations, all the while maintaining inward detachment from the role. There is a Sufi saying, "Be in the world, not of the world."

The Qur'an

A Muslim believes that the book known as the Qur'an is the word of Allah revealed to Prophet Muhammad. The Qur'an was dictated to the Prophet by the Angel Jibreel on various occasions throughout his lifetime to answer questions, solve problems, settle disputes and to be man's best guide to the truth. The Qur'an was revealed in Arabic and is still in its original, unchanged state today. One who has memorized the Qur'an may carry the title 'Hafiz.'

A Muslim also believes in a clear distinction between the Qur'an and the Traditions,

Hadith of the Prophet Muhammad. The Qur'an is the word of Allah, dictated to Muhammad, meant for all mankind. *Hadith*, the traditions of Prophet Muhammad, i.e. his teachings, sayings, and actions – the *Sunna* – are the practical interpretations of the Qur'an. The Qur'an and the Sunna of Prophet Muhammad are the primary sources of knowledge in Islam.

Hadith and Sunna of The Prophet

Hadith of the Prophet Muhammad have come to us in various forms, describing his sayings and his deeds and approval or disapproval of various actions or events. Looser interpretation of the term also may include narration by or about the Companions and Successors of the Prophet. Together these various texts are referred to as the Sunna, describing essentially how the Prophet lived his life.

Since *Hadith* literature is the other arm of Islamic thought, the rapid growth of Islam in the two centuries following the death of the Prophet understandably challenged Islamic scholars with two tasks:

1. to preserve this knowledge.

2. to identify and classify the large body of Hadith as to accuracy.

Thus the exacting science of Hadith evaluation and attribution came into being, the *Isnad*, a subject beyond the scope of this chapter, and your patience.

However, there is a special class of *Hadith*, called *Hadith Qudsi*. These are post-Qur'anic revelations from Allah related by the Prophet. Unlike the Prophet's comments on events or spirituality, these are received as if they were the word of God.

EARLY SUFIS

Prior to the 8th century A.D., Sufism was very much an internal, personal process. Following the example of the Prophet Muhammad, certain ascetic-minded Muslims began very rigorous self-training, making devotional prayers and solitary nocturnal vigils an integral part of their lives.

Famous mystics of this early period were Malik ibn Dinar (711-795) and Muhammad ibn Wasi (d.744 or 751). Malik ibn Dinar believed it was permitted to own a bit of land and be independent of men, while ibn Wasi believed it was better to not know where one's next meal would come from.

A famous woman saint of the time, Rabia al-Adawwiya (717-801), (also known as 'al-Basri'), elaborated on the Qur'anic theme of trust in God, through a series of remarkable ecstatic songs and poems, stressing purity of heart and the inner life. It is said that she used to kneel a thousand times daily saying, "I ask for no recompense but to satisfy the Almighty God." She also stated, "True devotion is for itself: not to desire Heaven nor to fear Hell."

This last is an important point, because devotion driven by fear is not devotion at all. Yet Suhrawardi (1155-1191) says, "Fear and hope are both necessary to prevent bad conduct."

The first mystic orders began to develop in the second century following the Advent of the Prophet, the 8th century A.D. The doctrine of annihilation (*Fana*) of the false self (*Nafs*) into Allah had taken root. This is the beginnings of a science of spirituality. Suhrawardi wrote:

> "The nafs is the root cause of human suffering and confusion and the enemy of individuation. It is the never satisfied, busy, tricky, fidgety monkey in a cage."

Sufis are fond of characterizing the uncontrolled *nafs* as an animal. It is more appropriate for the man to ride the donkey, than for the donkey to ride the man. In the Mathnavi (Masnavi, or Mathnawi), Rumi (1207-1273) tells the story of a bull who lived alone on a verdant island. Each night the bull would worry anxiously about the grass, since he'd eaten so much, what would he eat upon the morrow? Each morning of his life, there was plenty of grass to eat, but each night in the dark, unable to see the grass, he would start worrying again.

LEVELS OF THE FALSE SELF/EGO

Following is a short list of the levels of the false self/ego as defined by the Sufis.

• Commanding *Nafs* (*Nafs-i-Ammara*) In undeveloped man, this is the mechanism which drives one to indulge primitive satisfactions.

• Blaming/Accusatory *Nafs* (*Nafs-i-Lawwama*) When one's conscience is awakened, one cannot ignore certain matters of the heart.

• Inspired *Nafs* (*Nafs-i-Mulhama*) One raises one's sight to things spiritual and begins to live the ideal.

• Tranquil *Nafs* (*Nafs-i-Mutmaina*) One continuously contemplates the beauty of the Divine.

- Satisfied *Nafs* (*Nafs-i-Radziyya*) One accepts all that existence brings, remaining detached from anyone or anything than Allah.

- Satisfying *Nafs* (*Nafs-i-Mardiyyah*) One has arrived in a stage which is pleasing to Allah.

- Purified *Nafs* (*Nafs-i-Safiyyah, or Nafs al-Kamila*) One has no desire but is absorbed in the Truth – *Haqq*.

This list traces the evolution of the Self from cruelty to compassion and may be described as stations on the path, or *maqam*. The name of the *nafs* changes according to its function. Also, it seems to represent the process of recovery, as defined by modern psychotherapy.

There is a Hadith of the Prophet that when the Muslims returned from the battle of Tabuk, the Prophet said to them, "We are back from the minor battle and we are approaching the major one." They asked him, "What is that major *jihad*, O Messenger?" He replied, "Fighting against the ego (*nafs*)." This Hadith clearly shows the superiority of *jihadun nafs* (the struggle with the ego), which is the main aim of Sufism.

The Sufis are saying, loud and clear, that there are worlds and layers of development – even the possibility of divinity. This spiritual practice of surrender, scouring out of oneself, making room for the Divine, led the famous Sufi al-Bistami (804-874) to ecstatically proclaim,

> "Praise is to Me; how great is my majesty; I am your Lord," and "My banner is greater than that of Muhammad."

These outrageous statements were explained away as non- responsible and made in a state of God-intoxication:

> "A person who is in a state of ecstasy should not be rebuked for what he may utter in his ecstatic state."
> –Subayhi (d. 1038 est.)

The early Orders, and all that followed them, shared a characteristic: spiritual seekers clustered around an acknowledged teacher, following his example and absorbing the outward (*adab*) and inward (*ahwal*) states, in the same way that the Companions of the Prophet were changed by keeping company with him. Students of Sufism, *murids*, benefit profoundly from associating with a particular *murshid* – teacher or master – a pattern which continues to the present day.

To summarize the purpose, message, and methods developed by the early Sufis, the Qur'an described following the example of the Prophet Muhammad as 'purifying' for all mankind, and membership in a Sufi Order reflects this same method and purpose.

The heart states of Muhammad are not committed to books, but communicated from the knowers (*arifin*) to students. Because of the complexity of the task of surrender and spiritual growth, and the myriad beginning states or starting points of murids, the Sufis consider the only effective method of transmission of this spiritual science is the personal example of a living master.

SUFISM AND SHARIA

Sharia, Islamic Law

Together, the Qur'an and the Sunna are the basis for the religion of Islam. Sharia adds the use of interpretations of Muslim jurisprudence to the Qur'an and Sunna.

While Sharia may be taken as a set of ethical guidelines, in some Islamic countries Sharia is the actual rule of law. An inner as well as outer understanding of the letter and spirit of the Sharia is seen as crucial. Sufi and jurist ibn al-Arabi (1164-1240) once stated that the only jurist or *faqih* (one trained in jurisprudence) or *Ulema* that could serve well was a Friend of Allah, a *waliullah* (Sufi) who was also trained in ethical thinking. But ibn al-Arabi's standard for religious jurists has seldom been met. There is a Hadith of the Prophet:

> "Whoever among you outlives me shall see a vast dispute."

Man being man, there is always the danger of turning religion itself into a idolatrous net which insulates the practitioner, worried about legality of this or that act, from any possibility of experiencing the Divine. Within the Islamic tradition, the cure for this is Sufism.

In addition to the visible Order structure of murshid – murid relations and Sufi practices, the Sufis introduced a concept called "The Preserving Saints," which holds that the world is kept intact thanks to the existence of a network of corporeal or invisible saints of different ranks. These are some rungs of this spiritual ladder: *Awtad* or pegs, people who can communicate with Perfect Masters across space and time; *Abdal*, or Successors, can appear and disappear anywhere on earth; next are the *Am'aid* or pillars. All of these connections terminate in a being, the *Qutb*, which is the pole or axis around which the whole universe rotates. If not for this structure, the Sufis believe the universe would go to pieces.

A special place in this spiritual hierarchy (the online Webster's Dictionary has this as the first definition of 'hierarchy': "a division of angels") is occupied by al-Khidr (sometimes

'Khizr'), the Green Saint, who some say is immortal, or possesses the water of Life, and whose function it is to guide those in need, those without access to a living teacher.

Some traditions say that al-Khidr is the prophet Elijah from the Old Testament. Many eminent Sufis claim to have received knowledge directly from al-Khidr. He is deemed to be a special 'Servant of God' as described in the Qur'an Sura 18:60-82, where he is described as spiritual guide to Moses. Meher Baba (1894-1969) indicated that Saint Francis benefitted from contact with al-Khidr.

One of the main tenets of Islam is the Kalimah, the statement *La ilaha illa Allah*, "There is No God but Allah." Within Islam, this monotheist concept is called *Tawhid* – to believe that there is no partner to Allah in His being and in His attributes. Alternatively, a major sin within Islam is called *shirk*, defined as putting anything, or anyone, on a level with Allah. Divinity cannot be given to Man, including the Prophet, who was known as the Messenger. As Man is slave to Allah, believing that Man can become divine is considered *shirk*.

Contrast this to the concept of The Preserving Saints and reverence and belief in both the *Qutb* and al-Khidr, and we have now arrived at the point where some Sufi beliefs and statements appear to constitute heresy.

In Islam, though there is not officially an intermediary between the Muslim and Allah, the jurist class, the *Ulema*, condemned some of the early Sufis and their practices as 'innovations' and therefore suspect, if not outright heretic. A famous Sufi, Mansur al-Hallaj (858-922), was executed in Baghdad for consistently stating, *Ana al-Haqq*, "I am the Truth."

He also insisted that Jesus had been a Sufi master, which somehow labelled Hallaj as a secret Christian, and therefore a *kaffir*, or unbeliever, even though both the Qur'an and various Hadith repeatedly honor Jesus and Mary. Dhu-Nun al-Misri, the Egyptian (796-859), credited with classifying the stages of spiritual development, was charged with heresy by the *Ulema* in Baghdad in 854 A.D.

Early Sufi masters al-Junayd (835-910) and al-Ghazzali (1058-IIII) did much to legitimize Sufi practice. Muhammad al-Ghazzali, around 1095, wrote several works which managed to reconcile intellectual, traditional Islamist, and Sufi mystic elements. Al-Ghazzali erased many of the objections that orthodox Islamic jurists had to the Sufi Orders, by reinterpreting Qur'anic verses and pointing out the interior meaning of many of the *Hadith*. For example, there is a *Hadith Qudsi* where the Prophet explained that Allah has stated:

> "When my Slave becomes My beloved, I become his ears through which he listens, his eyes through which he sees, his hands by which he holds, his feet by which he walks. When he pleads to Me for anything I definitely bestow it on him. When he seeks refuge in Me from any bad deed, then I definitely save him from it."

The Qur'an contains instructions suitable to man with varying levels of spirituality. It satisfies those who are content with merely exoteric practices, but also contains the deepest and most profound esoteric meaning for those who desire a closer, more mystical relationship with God.

One Qur'anic verse which is a favorite of the Sufis:

"Allah is closer to man than his own jugular vein." 50.16

To this day there is still shouting from those who believe the science of Sufism to be *bid'aa*, a reprehensible innovation, clearly involving saint worship and 'intermediaries' between man and Allah and therefore is *shirk* and outside Islam. Sufis consider those people to be externalists and primarily concerned with appearances, not the cleanliness of their own souls.

However, this fundamentalist anti-Sufi attitude is far from universal. Many Muslim communities around the world have historically and to this day consider membership in an order to be a normal part of life. Traditional Muslim Sufis are very devout and adhere closely to Islamic law as defined in the Qur'an and Hadith, considering this activity the starting point, not the ending, of their spirituality.

Rumi, founder of the Mevlevi Sufi order, wrote:

> "I am the slave of the Qur'an for as long as I am living. I am dust on the path of Muhammad, the Chosen One."

SUFI ORDERS

SILSILA CONCEPT

The Arabic word *silsila* means 'chain,' or continuity of personal transmission of esoteric knowledge.

A Sufi student is initiated into an Order by a Sufi master. The master's authority has been passed to him by a previous master, through the investiture of the traditional mantle of authority, symbolized by the presentation of a cloak of patched cloth, or *khirqa*. This initiation is supported by the chain of lineage going back through all the previous masters to the Prophet Muhammad, from whom the authority to instruct in the esoteric doctrine originated. Even today, this is the general practice of all the recognized Sufi orders. Each *murshid* can present a written list of his spiritual lineage, going back to the Prophet and the Angel Jibreel (Gabriel). Who is on these lists? There is a *hadith* from the Prophet which states,

"I am the city of knowledge and Ali is the door to it."

Ali (600-661) was the son-in-law of the Prophet, and was one of the first Muslim converts. Because of his courage as a very young man, Ali is known as the Lion of Islam. Ali had four Khalifs, or lieutenants: Hassan (624-670), Hussain (626-680), Kumayl (622-706), and Hassan Basri (642-728).

The first formal Silsila was founded by Abdul Wahid bin Zayd (711-793) who was a Khalifa of Hassan Basri. Bin Zayd passed away 171 years after the Prophet's *Hijira* to Medina, or 793. (Rabia al-Adawwiya, mentioned earlier, also known as Rabia al-Basri, was a contemporary of Hassan Basri.)

The earliest Sufi orders began very close to the Prophet's lifetime, with knowledge and instruction communicated from him to Ali, and then from Ali personally to the various Khalifs. There are 14 main and formal *silsilas*, or Orders. All of these originated from Ali. Later, these Orders expanded into more than 40 separate groups. Each order has at all times a *Shaikh-ul-Mashaikh*, or living leader.

There are two main branches of Islam, the Sunni and the Shia. When the Prophet Muhammad passed on in 632, there was dissension in the Muslim community regarding whether he had designated a successor. Some of the Companions believed he had clearly stated that Ali, his son-in-law and nephew, should be the leader, or *Imam*. Tradition, however, swayed the majority of the community, and Abu Bakr (573-634), an old friend of the Prophet's, was elected as the first Caliph, first leader of the Sunni movement. The other group believed that Ali and the family and descendants of the Prophet were his legitimate temporal and spiritual successors. This group is known as Shi'ati Ali, the supporters of Ali, or the Shia. An individual in this group is a Shi'ite. Estimates of Shia among Muslims worldwide range from 15 to 20 percent, concentrated mostly in Iran and Iraq.

A sorry series of events occurred in the Muslim community within thirty years of the Prophet's death—attempted and completed assassinations, all the way to open warfare.

Just as there are Sunni and Shia Muslims, it follows that there are Sunni and Shia Sufi orders. Shia Sufi orders such as the Nimatullahi have Hazrat Ali in their written Silsila, immediately following the Prophet. Surprisingly, all the Sunni orders do as well, except the Naqshbandi/Haqqani, who mention the first Caliph, Abu Bakr, not Ali, in their written Silsila. With this exception, it is clear then that 1400 years of both Sunni and Shia Sufis consider that Caliph Ali was given something not given to the other Companions, something vital to the spiritual development of man. Yet the vast majority of Sufi orders say, "We are Sunni", i.e. religious followers of the way of Abu Bakr.

Here is the beginning of the *silsila* for the Chishti Order, (Sunni):

- Hazrat Jibra'il (the Angel Gabriel)
- Hazrat Khwaja Muhammad Rasul Allah (The Prophet)
- Hazrat Khwaja 'Ali Wali Allah (the fourth Caliph of Islam, Ali)
- Hazrat Khwaja Hasan Basri (Ali's Khalif)
- Hazrat Khwaja 'Abd al-Wahid bin Zayd (founder of the first Order)
- Hazrat Khwaja Fuzayl bin 'Iyaz.

Here is the beginning of the *silsila* for the Naqshbandi Order (Sunni):

- Muhammad ibn Abd Allah (The Prophet)
- Abu Bakr as- Siddiq (the first Caliph of Islam)
- Salman al-Farsi ('The Persian,' a Companion)
- Qassim ibn Muhammad ibn Abu Bakr (grandson of Abu Bakr)
- Jafar as-Sadiq (sixth Shi'ite Imam)
- Tayfur Abu Byazid al-Bistami (originator of term *Fana*)

A Sufi order grows from the personality and training methods of the founder of the order, the original Shaikh. The Orders also take on the characteristics of the people involved in them; there is a huge difference between the methods of the quiet, sober, deadly earnest Naqshbandis of the Middle East and the wild, exuberant Rifai of North Africa.

The goal is the same, however — annihilation of the false self into Allah. The visible effect is to reach a state of inner equilibrium where no importance is attached to either praise or blame, failure or success.

The Heart

A Muslim's five daily prayers, *salat*, involve certain recitations and prostrations in the direction of Mecca. These recitations and prostrations are called *rakats*, and are meaningful to the Sufi in part because this prostration is the only time one's heart is above one's head.

A passive, in pain being with a broken heart is useless to Sufi order or to themselves. The murshid has the delicate task of slowly breaking the lifelong accretions around the human heart without causing permanent, debilitating emotional damage to the student, allowing them to love fully, freely and intuitively.

Love is both the message and the method of imparting the message. Since Sufis allude to nonverbal and distant communication between practitioners, the outsider must imagine the attunement, alignment and intuition necessary between these people for any sort of reliable connection or message passing. The hidden, unspoken and unseen connection between an advanced *murshid* and *murid* or *mutawassit* well along in the work can only be discussed in terms of Love. This direct transmission is called *tawaj* by Naqshbandis.

This heart-to-heart *rab'ta* (*rabita*) is also called *tassawur-I-shaykh*, 'blending with the Shaykh.' It is a non-romantic but burningly intense love between *murid* and teacher, love that the murshid attempts to transfer higher in the *silsila*—the *murid's* Fana-fi Murshid becomes Fana-fi Shaikh (the founder of the Order), then to the Prophet, then to the goal, to Allah, Fana-fillah.

Look at the issue of communication from the reverse angle. Assume that a murid misses an important signal or direction transmitted from the murshid. Since the murid missed it and therefore did not act upon it, there is no sense of having failed at a task, since each task actually begins by perceiving it. A very subtle and ultimately kind filtration system.

Rabita or *tawaj* may also exist between advanced Sufis, regardless of order, location, or time. The Sufi asserts that the founders of the Orders may still be contacted directly. Taking this further, Suhrawardi (1144-1234) and the Shia Sufis of Iran, the so-called Isfahan School, discussed and prepared for sudden illumination from above by systematically purifying themselves. This science of direct cognition or 'knowledge by presence' is called by them *ilm al-huduri.*

While it is relatively simple to mention and define states and methods and teachers and Orders, calling Sufism the 'science of spirituality,' the dimension of Love is necessarily far more difficult to access, understand, and explain.

Disciples come for knowledge, devotees come for Love. It is better to come for Love.

THE TRUE TEACHER

A *murshid*, or *pir*, or *shaykh*, is not the founder of an order. He has risen through the ranks, as *khalifa*, or lieutenant, has received the *khirqa*, or mantle, from an acknowledged murshid, and later may be granted permission to take murids and begin a branch of the order, if he so chooses and conditions are right. At that point that person is referred to as *murshid*, or teacher.

There are in fact formal qualifications for a murshid. Most Sufi Orders have the tradition of a written 'license to practice,' called *ijaza nama*. The *ijaza nama* specifies the duties and responsibilities of the murshid as given by his own Shaykh, plus one or more complete *silsila* records (depending on how many orders to which the new murshid belongs) – tracing the spiritual lineage back to the Prophet and (with noted exceptions) to Caliph Ali. Simply having the license does not mean the bearer is a perfected teacher, a *kamil shaykh*.

A *kamil shaykh* is considered to possess:

- Knowledge of the Sharia, Qur'an, Hadith, and Islamic jurisprudence

- Expertise in the rites and rituals of his particular order

- Practical knowledge of the stations – *maqqamat* – that mark the progress of a murid

- Personal experience with the stages of Fana, annihalation of the false self

- Continuous inner bonding – *rab'ta* – with his own *murshid*, and with the founder of his own order, and with the Prophet Muhammad

Some would-be students of Sufism are not aware that their motives include the wish for exotic, unusual experience, or are motivated by what can only be called spiritual greed. The teacher must provide a real context in which each *murid* can grow at his or her best pace. The teacher is not there to provide psychotherapy to the *murid*, but to adjust and open perceptions far beyond psychotherapy's scope. The teacher must be able to diagnose the stage of the pupil, and the learner must come to the stage where he can accept this without resentment or pride. Beyond this, the true *murshid* strives to make himself irrelevant – except in inner connection – to the *murid*. Rumi says:

> "Wool, through the presence of a man of knowledge, becomes a carpet. Earth and stone may become a palace. The presence of a spiritual man creates a similar transformation."

Alchemy, in other words. Base materials become fine, and useful. But how to recognize the true teacher? The proof of the teacher is in the quality, nature, and accomplishments – the refinement of heart and mind – of the students. The Sufi master ibn al-Arabi stated,

> "People think that a teacher should display miracles and manifest illumination. But the requirement in a teacher is that he should possess all that the disciple needs."

Because spirituality works and expresses on the intuitive level, the opportunities to choose poorly are many. While one would hope that the *silsila* and investiture ceremonies and even possession of an *ijaza nama* would eliminate them, there are as many false teachers in Sufism as in other spiritual disciplines.

The problem is compounded because of the Sufi's disregard for externals. A seeker may encounter a false teacher who takes pains to look and act the part, and therefore appears genuine, while a *kamil shaykh* with real knowledge is avoided, because he does not match the seeker's immature idea of how a spiritual teacher should look and act. Many teaching-stories involve a teacher acting in a non-spiritual or irreligious manner, scaring off the unready. This process frees the genuine master of the task of dismissing indiscriminating, incapable would-be *murids*; misled by externals, these people dismiss themselves in advance.

An elegant system.

Murid-Murshid Pact

Love is both the door and the key to the door.

Someone first encountering Sufism by reading would imagine that its prime reason for existing is to train new Sufis.

There is in fact a formalized relationship between the teacher, known as a *murshid*, and the aspirant, called the *murid*, as well as a course of study. While these connections may last a lifetime, it is also possible that an individual may require exposure to other teaching methods in different areas of the world. Travel and apprenticeship have historically been part of the Sufi Way. Because of special training, the aspirant's inner states are readily apparent to the advanced Sufi.

Sufism utilizes a codified, systematic gradation of the various stages of spiritual development. These terms and definitions are usually in Arabic, and may be expressed in varying degrees of *fana*, meaning absorption or obliteration. The duty of the student is to obliterate the *nafs*, or false self, into the *murshid*. This state is called *Fana-fi Murshid*. Then the aspirant is handed up the chain to the founder of the Sufi Order in which the *murid* is enrolled. This state is called *Fana-fi Shaikh*. Final states are known as *Fana-fi Rasul*, absorption into the Prophet Muhammad, then *Fana-Fillah*, into Allah, the Creator. Advanced indeed.

As Allah is pure light (*Nur*) and energy, without preparation and the guidance of an (illumined) teacher, any touch of that true Reality (*haqiqa*) would drive a person of ordinary consciousness insane. There are in fact in the East some persons known as *mahdzubs* or *masts*, who have in a sense gone too far too fast without guidance, and are absorbed in Allah and have withdrawn or are unable to perform normal social functions. By Western standards they would be considered insane. Because of this, Sufi training systematically creates heavier and heavier emotional and mental circuitry, so the practitioner may participate in this world without being overwhelmed by a higher plane of consciousness.

The connection between the student and *murshid* is all-important, and each has a set of obligations or duty toward the other.

Duties of the Murid

It is said that human beings utilize only about five to seven percent of their estimated mental capability. Because Sufism is, in one dimension, the science of developing higher human functions and consciousness, it requires candidates with extraordinary aptitudes coupled with a humble inner demeanor.

However, it should be acknowledged that would-be *murids* may appear before a *murshid* in a very imperfect, incomplete state. If they have that spark within them the teacher can, in time, help them transform into genuine students with real capabilities, balanced beings, and paradoxically having no greed for spiritual, exotic experience or special powers. Life's polishing away of undesirable blocking traits is normally, even naturally, seen as misfortune, events to be avoided. These are the very experiences which work on the *nafs* and are therefore embraced by the aspirant. So we are told.

In *Kitab adab al-Muridin* (A Sufi Rule For Novices), Suhrawardi says,

"...the first duty of a student of Sufism is that the student must make himself inwardly clean."

This means he must be able to operate without the distorting effects of anger, greed, envy, and so on, which are regarded by Sufis as pre-human; monkeys and other animals exhibit all of these qualities on occasion.

The second duty is to have worldly interests, but to do one's best to not be attached to the results, and reach a state where apparent success or failure are truly seen as equal. Sufis say the proper attitude is "In the world, not of the world."

The third duty is submission to the murshid as part of a contract of mutual and total respect. Knowledge cannot be gained except in an attitude of humble openness.

The fourth duty is to follow a course of study prescribed by the *murshid* in the order recommended. Another is to understand the relative ranking of the various studies and to know the connections, so one doesn't concentrate on the irrelevant. A further duty of the student of Sufism is that the aim should be self-effacement, not visible power or influence.

Sufism is a polishing process, the loss of the ego/false self, in order to make room for that eventual, sacred Addition.

AMONG THE SLEEPING

TEACHING METHODS

Zikr

The Sufis live with an ever increasing awareness of God. One aspect of this awareness is the practice of *zikr*, sometimes spelled *dhikr*, which means 'remembering God.' One pronounces one or more of Allah's Names or attributes or utters a number of recognized formulae. The *murshid* usually assigns a phrase and a number of required repetitions.

The Qur'an repeatedly admonishes believers to celebrate the praises of God and to do this often. Some Sufis (notably the Naqshbandi) do constant *wazifa*, which is the internal, silent repetition of *zikr* phrases. The following verse of the Qur'an reveals the significance of *zikr*:

"Recite that which has been revealed to you of the scripture, and observe prayer. For prayer restrains one from lewdness and iniquity, but remembrance of God is the greatest virtue." 29.45

In a passage of the Qur'an, the importance of *zikr* is emphasized to such an extent that a response from God is assured:

> "Therefore remember Me, and I will remember you." 2.152

A Hadith in support of the practice: "Allah did not listen to anything as He listened to *zikr* recitation by a prophet with a nice voice."

Sufis take the word 'remembrance' in the Qur'an to mandate the practice of *zikr*. Dr. Talat Halman recounted this story of the Prophet 'prescribing' *zikr*:

> In a very popular *hadith* narrated by Hazrat 'Ali, Fatima, the Prophet's daughter, once asked the Prophet for a servant, a request which he declined. That night he came to her house and told her he was giving her something better than a servant: "Say *subhanallah* (God is perfect) 33 times, *al-hamdu li-'llah* (all praise to God) 33 times, and *Allahu Ak-*

bar (God is most great) 34 times." This *zikr*, typically and frequently done after *salat* (prayer) is called the 'Tasbih Fatima Glorification of [as in given to] Fatima.'

THE FIRST KALIMAH

The *Kalimah*, the basic Islamic statement of belief, is: *'La ilaha illa Allah wa Muhammad ar-Rasul Allah'*.

"There is no God/deity but Allah and Muhammad is his messenger."

The phrase *'La ilaha illa Allah'* is one of the most commonly used phrases in *zikr*. This phrase consciously affirms there is no deity besides Allah. On the surface this means to beware of idols, false prophets, money, prestige and power, but taken farther – and the Sufi always takes it farther – to deny one's own ego (justifying the *fana* process of *nafs*-obliteration), and denying the apparent supremacy of physical reality. This what Hindus and Vedantists refer to as *maya*, the illusion of physical reality – and the illusion of time. Quantum physics has also questioned the existence of time and physical reality. Albert Einstein (1879 - 1955), physicist and mathematician, said:

> "The difference between the past, the present and the future is only a persistent illusion."

However, once one has negated everything except Allah, how can we possibly reach Him?

The last section of the *Kalimah*, *'Muhammad ar-Rasul Allah'*, "(and) Muhammad is the Prophet – or messenger – of Allah" kindly tells us that the Prophet Muhammad is the conduit or connection to Allah – the Prophet is the available bridge between the tangible and the intangible.

Therefore, learning and living the states the Prophet experienced is the goal of the Sufi teaching and the purpose of the Orders. This is expressly why each major order is so conscious of its *silsila*, the chain of personal, living transmission of knowledge and experience, going back to Caliph Ali and the Prophet.

SAMA

The term *sama* means 'hearing' or 'audition.' Two of the Orders, the Mevlevi of Turkey, and the Chistis in Pakistan and India, utilize a combination of *zikr*, music, and dance to create the possibility of creating a *hal* state for the participants, which may include visions and loss of normal consciousness. In Suhrawardi's 'A Sufi Rule For Novices,' Sufi master Junayd defines *hal* as:

> "..a form of inspiration which comes down to the heart but does not stay in it permanently."

The *murshid* or *shaikh* connects the state and aspiration (*jam al-himma*) of the listeners and dancers with the energy of the musicians, and may grant the experience.

However, knowing how easily the human organism can become addicted to the unusual, the exotic, some teachers discourage repeat experiences:

"If a novice is attracted to *sama*, you can know there is still in him a remainder of falseness." – Junayd

Teaching Stories

Sufi *murshids* have traditionally used teaching-stories as a part of the process of awakening the student. Study of these stories can lead to an intimate knowledge of cause and effect in the practitioner. While many of the stories have an obvious moral, for example, or a clever twist of logic which the acute reader may appreciate, it is held that many of these stories, considered in proper order and at appropriate length, will help the snail leave its shell. There is a Sufi aphorism, *Al mujazu qantarat al-Haqiqa* – 'The Relative is a channel to the Truth.'

George Bernard Shaw (1856-1950) said, "When a thing is funny, search it for a hidden truth." Mullah Nasruddin is an internationally known mythic figure, the Fool of God, used in many Sufi teaching-stories. These often uncover unconscious assumptions in the listener. Sometimes the logical fallacy in the story is meant to shock the listener into a different mind-space.

A MULLAH NASRUDDIN STORY

As a young man, Nasrudin went to his shaykh asking him for advice and blessings. The old sage said, "I will offer you some words of wisdom that will provide you with a source of guidance for the rest of your life, if only you know how to use them." Nasrudin nodded eagerly.

"Always remember," the Shaykh said, "life is like a fountain."

Nasrudin pondered the *shaykh's* words carefully. Thirty years later, he received a letter informing him that his teacher was on his deathbed. Knowing that this was his final chance to see his *shaykh*, Nasrudin rushed to his beloved teacher's side. "*Mawlana*," began Nasrudin with a heavy heart, "I have but one question to ask of you. For over three decades now, whenever I fell upon hard times, or was sad or confused, I thought about the phrase you passed on to me, and it has helped me through many difficult times. But to be perfectly honest, I have never entirely grasped its implications nor fully understood its meaning. Now that you are about to enter the realm of truth, tell me, my dear teacher, why is life like a fountain?"

"Alright, alright," replied the old man wearily, "so it's not like a fountain!"

ANOTHER NASRUDDIN STORY

Once Nasruddin went to a garden and climbed an apricot tree. The gardener observed this and asked him, "Why have you climbed my master's tree?" Nasruddin answered, "I am a nightingale, and for nightingales climbing a tree is not a sin." The gardener said, "Then please sing so I may listen and enjoy." Nasruddin started to sing in his hoarse voice. The gardener asked him, "Why would a nightingale sing so badly?" Nasruddin replied, "A nightingale which eats raw apricots will never sing better than this."

AND ANOTHER NASRUDDIN STORY

Nasruddin used to stand in the street on market days, to be pointed out as an idiot. No matter how often people offered him a large and a small coin, he always chose the smaller piece. One day a kindly man said to him, "Nasruddin, you should take the bigger coin. Then you will have more money and people will no longer be able to make a laughing stock of you." "That may be true," said Nasruddin, "but if I take the larger coin just once, people will stop offering me money."

A STORY ILLUSTRATING AN UNCONVENTIONAL ESCAPE

An Iranian Sufi *shaykh* was a rather handsome man and many women were interested in him. A certain woman tried everything she could think of to draw the attention of the *shaykh*, but he was not in love with her. Then she had him kidnapped. When he was in her power, he said that he would marry her. But first, he wished to use the bathroom. The woman allowed him to go. He returned after shaving not only his beard off, but also his eyebrows and all the hair on his face. She was disgusted with his appearance and let him go.

A FABLE (NOT NECESSARILY FUNNY)

Once Upon A Time there was a country with a very strange custom. Any man could become king, but only for five years. At the end of that time soldiers would come, tie the king up, take him to a certain wild island full of fearsome beasts, and leave him there.

So king after king for generations had parties, married many women, indulged themselves completely, and were very happy. Until the five years were up. Then off they were carried, crying and screaming, to the island of wild beasts.

Then one day a young man volunteered to become king. But this young king was different. Instead of squandering the country's wealth on parties, or marriages, he enlisted farmers to journey to the island and clear some land. He hired hunters to kill many of the wild beasts that lived there. He employed builders to create a small village at the edge of the farmland. And toward the end he sent his family to move into this village.

At the end of five years he was packed off to the island, not screaming and crying, but with a wide smile upon his face.

Poetry

Sufi poetry was not written as entertainment. Read in the original Persian or Arabic by a prepared student of mysticism, the best Sufi poetry can help the *murid's* spiritual progress. Most of the imagery and metaphors come from the character. As beauty (*jamal*) and majesty (*jalal*) usually accompany one another, Rumi often mentions the thorn with the Rose.

The Wine is the intoxication of divine Love (*jadhba*). This image is used deliberately, in an abstinent Muslim society, to make it clear that the absorption of the dervish in Allah is not simple emotionality. Drunken men tend to dance, as in the Mevlevi *sama*, so the Wine and the Dance go hand in hand. The Tavern is the world, and yet Wine is readily available in the Tavern.

> A drunkard wasted away on
> Love's way
> His sweet drunken slumber
> Is profoundest prayer.
> —'Iraqi (1213-1289)

Upon that station that lovers,
With her lip in mind, drink wine,
Uncouth is the drunkard conscious of himself.
—'Hafiz (1326-1390)

None but the drunkard knows
The tavern's secrets —
How could the sober understand
The mysteries of that street!
—'Iraqi

A recurring theme in Sufi poetry and teaching is the 'treasure in the ,' sometimes the 'Tavern Of Ruin' — *kharabat*. The message is that you must ruthlessly tear down your house, or the tavern, to the last stone, because there is a treasure in the foundation. This metaphor represents the gradual eradication of the false self, in which all external attachment falls away, leaving the treasure, a surrendered, winged heart.

Famous Sufi poets include Fariddudin Attar (1145-1221), Hafiz, Jami (1414-1492), Jelalludin Rumi (1207-1273), Saadi of Shiraz (1210-1292 est.), Fakhr al-Din 'Iraqi and Shabistari (1288-1340). Finding readable translations which have not been drained of the essence is a difficult but extremely rewarding task.

BARAKA

Baraka is not actually a teaching method but a product of directed Sufi work. Depending upon circumstances, or those involved, *baraka* may be perceived as a blessing, or energy, or benefit, or message, or personal power, or charisma. The Sufi Order is in one sense a channel for *baraka*. Its manifestation may be invisible to a conditioned mind, accustomed to expect near immediate results for effort.

A STORY FROM RUMI
ILLUSTRATING BARAKA IN ACTION

Two beggars came to the door of a house, asking for bread. One was immediately given some bread, and went away satisfied. The second was kept waiting, and waiting. Why? The first beggar was not greatly liked, and was given a small piece of stale bread. The second was made to wait while a fresh loaf of bread was baked for him.

This kind of story illustrates the temporal and causal disconnects which make a conditioned mind assume that nothing is happening, because the real, behind the scenes activity is not apparent to him.

A story from master Fariduddin Attar (in his manuscript "Recitals of the Saints"):

The great Sufi Habib Ajami (d.737 or 757, est.), when he went to a river to wash, left his coat upon the ground. Hasan of Basra was passing by and saw it. Thinking that someone should look after this property, he stood guard over it until Habib Ajami returned. Hasan asked Habib whom he had left looking after the coat. "In the care," said Habib, "of He who gave you the task of looking after it!"

INTERCESSION

Sufi literature is peppered with miracle stories in which the founder of an order, or some *murshid* or *shaykh*, benefits a person or community indirectly or by spiritual or magical means. Among Sufis, a part of the process is often a visit to a tomb- shrine, perhaps the founder of the Order, or another venerated by the Order.

These tomb visits, called *'ziyarat'*, have an effect in direct proportion to the spiritual intention of the visitor, and should not be confused with *hajj*, the major pilgrimage to Mecca, a required rite performed at a fixed time each year.

The question naturally arises, how is this issue treated within the Muslim community? What is the attitude towards the supplication to a pious person, and why is this not considered *'shirk'*? If the resulting benefit appears to be supernatural in origin, why is it not considered witchcraft?

There are three *hadiths* from the Companions about the actions and life of the Prophet which serve to 'normalize' the situation:

1. `Uthman ibn `Abdullah said: "My wife sent me to Umm Salama (one of the Prophet's wives) with a cup of water in which to dip a lock containing some of the Prophet's hair. Whenever a person was suffering from the evil eye or an illness, they would send her a vessel of water (for this). I looked into (it) and saw some red hairs." (The Prophet was red-headed.)

2. Abu Musa related that "The Prophet called for a vessel of water, washed his hands and face in it, spat a mouthful of water back into it and then said to Abu Musa and Bilal, 'drink from it and pour the rest over your faces and chests.' "

3. Mahmud ibn Rabi` said that "when the Prophet performed his ablution, the Companions almost fought over the excess water."

Each of these Hadith demonstrates that it is permissible to obtain blessings through someone who is closer to Allah than oneself. Because of the Prophet's personal impeccability, there was no taint of 'shirk', in that he did not consider that the blessings emanated from anywhere or anyone except Allah. And because the channel for these blessings was the Prophet himself, Muslims continued the tradition of seeking blessings through *awliya* – saints.

Seeking the blessing from a saintly person is not the same at all as worshipping them, a distinction that is not always clear among detractors of the Sufi orders.

AMONG THE SLEEPING

The Real Work may not be educating junior Sufis at all. While the Sufi Work depends on a populace of evolved practitioners, teaching is by no means the most important function of the Sufi hierarchy, historically or in the present day.

One favorite *hadith* of the Sufis is,

"Human beings are asleep, and when they die they will awaken."

This Hadith's apparent meaning is that all will become clear upon our death. A deeper meaning is that the mass of mankind is in a deep hypnotic state in which physical reality is all, intuition is seen as unreliable, security equates to a large family and/or money in the bank, and religion is an obligation, necessary for social standing.

The Prophet also said, "Die before you die," which opens the possibility of awakening to our true nature and relation to the Creator while still alive. The Sufi considers that 'sleep' mentioned in the *hadith* above is the deep illusion resulting from the Real Self being veiled by the False Self. The 'death' is the death of the False Self, or *nafs*. The Sufi Hakim Sanai (d. 1141 est.) wrote:

> "Everyone in the ordinary world is asleep. Their religion – the religion of the familiar world – is emptiness, not religion at all."

While Sufism does indeed aim to assist the properly motivated and capable human to awaken, i.e. training of *murids*, it has a parallel and deadly serious purpose. Earlier, certain spiritual personages were mentioned, the *Awtad* and the *Abdal*. The number of these people vary, and they are assigned to specific locales, depending on the area's history, population, and overall state of spiritual readiness. They may or may not reside in the area for which they are responsible. They have specific duties. Sufis would say that in addition to helping members to rise, the Sufi Work includes two other main phases: absorption of the negative emanations from entire sleeping populations and distribution of positive emanations from Allah to those sleeping populations.

This leads to an outrageous statement, nonetheless a core belief of Sufis and of those associated with Sufis – without this absorption of "evil" and dissemination of "good" performed by the corporeal Sufi Orders along with the hierarchy of Sufi Preserving Saints, humanity would have ceased to be long ago.

In that sense advanced Sufis benefit everyone in the world, whether they know it or not. These self-sacrificing advanced beings deserve our deepest possible gratitude.

This is a secret that is concealed by its very improbability.

Among the Sleeping

MORE QUESTIONS AND ANSWERS

DISCUSS 'FANA' AND 'BAQA.'

So far, this book has been peppered with references to *fana*, or 'absorption'. Also used to mean obliteration or annihilation of the false self. This happens in stages. The term, and state, refer to the stages of growth of a *murid* in an Order. The *murid becomes* absorbed, blended into the *murshid*, then *becomes* obliterated into the founder of the order, then *becomes*... A process of always *becoming*, journeying from one state to another.

Every journey reaches an end point. The final *fana*, the target, the goal, is *Fanafillah*, being one with God. Sufis use a different term after *Fanafillah* is achieved, for the one who has arrived, *baqa*. One translation is 'abiding.'

The literal meaning of *baqa* in Arabic is permanence, or subsistence-in. The 'Dictionary of Spiritual Terms' states *baqa* is:

> "...the spiritual state of subsistence beyond all form, i.e. the state of reintegration in the Spirit, or even in pure Being; also means the Divine Eternity. Its opposite is *fanā*'."

We're right up against the limits of language here. A repeat of a statement from the introduction:

> Any discussion of Sufism is further complicated by the fact that words are themselves metaphors, mere stand- ins for the real thing or experience; the meaning derived from reading a sequence of words is utterly dependent upon the experience of the person reading them.

DISCUSS 'EXOTERIC' AND 'ESOTERIC.'

There are twenty-two special verses in the Qur'an's Sura 18, 'The Cave,' 60 through 82. These illustrate the gulf between the exoteric, everyday interpretation of events, the 'normal' perception of sleeping humanity, and the esoteric, deeper, far more accurate and prescient knowledge of the *wali-ullah*, the Friend of God.

Verses 60-82 describe the Green Saint, Khidr, encountering Moses, who asked to follow Khidr and learn from him. Khidr responded that Moses would 'not be able to have patience' with him. Moses persisted and then five short tales follow. In each of these, Khidr made incomprehensible decisions and commited horrible-looking acts, including murder. Moses protested at each occurrence, demonstrating the shallow surface observation and judgment of the unawakened. In each instance Khidr revealed the unknown background of each, the deeper import of the events, and the ultimate reason for his acts. Moses was literally blind to all these aspects, showing in high relief the gulf of understanding and the difference between observation and true knowing.

Excusing murder? Surely this can't represent wisdom and oneness with God. A verse from a poem of Rumi:

"...Beyond ideas of wrongdoing and rightdoing, there is a field. I'll meet you there."

The gulf between normal morality and the insight of the *waliullah* seems unbridgeable. This has cropped up over and over in interactions between Sufis and the jurist class, the *Ulema*. *Sharia* was assembled by the Muslim community from the Qur'an and the *Sunna* - the *hadith* - of the Prophet and Companions. Muslims following Sharia accepted it as a Way and a Path. But the cultural norm in that culture was that the highest aspiration of the Muslim was to achieve slave status, a dedicated servant of God, an *Ab'dul Allah*, an *Abdullah*.

Knowing his culture, the Prophet was careful to limit his claim to being the Messenger of God. Ali and his *khalifs*, the first Sufis, realized if *Sharia* is a path, a Way, there must then be a Goal. The secret the Sufis preserve to the present day is that the goal - to realize the heart-states of the Prophet in one's own life - is nothing less than the seventh plane: God-realization.

For this reason, Sufis have often borne the brunt of mainstream Muslim persecution in both Sunni and Shia environments, on the grounds of *shirk*, claiming that anyone or anything could be on the level of Allah. Sufi Mansur al-Hallaj was tortured and killed for saying, "I am the Truth." 'Truth,' *al-Haqq*, is one of the ninety-nine names or characteristics of God, and that was enough.

Many deep thanks to Laurent Weichberger and Dan Sanders for providing many of these thought-provoking questions.

Among the Sleeping

SUFISM WITHOUT ISLAM

Because a thorough understanding and practice of the *Shariat* of Islam is seen as an inextricable aspect of and prerequisite for correctly practicing Sufism, those in the Eastern, traditional orders often have a problem with the legitimacy of orders mostly stripped of Islamic practices.

THE INAYATI

There are many Westernized Sufi orders, most notably various offshoots from the Indian Chishti Hazrat Inayat Khan (1882-1927), who brought Sufism to Europe and the United States in the early years of the twentieth century. While the teaching methods are similar, working with the names of God, employing *zikr* in the original Arabic, etc., it is nonetheless true that Inayat Khan's teachings, in the hands of the various offshoot Orders, American and European, do not make traditional Islamic practices mandatory.

How is this viewed in the East? In an e-mail interview for this chapter, a Khalifa in the Silsila Siraajiya Haqqaaniya (a Chishti offshoot) in Lahore, Pakistan, stated:

> "As far as Inayat Khan sahib is concerned, we have serious doubts that the Sufis dislike him because they do not give their opinion on the basis of incomplete information and there is not enough information available about him. We do not think that he stripped strict Islamic practice (prayer, fasting etc) from his teachings.
>
> The Sufis have always believed that a nonMuslim *Murid* will convert due to the *Suhba* (*Murshid's* speech at gatherings) as the Murshid is the role model for him/her. They prefer conversion out of love instead of forcing the conversion. In case someone does not accept Islam, we believe that he/she will not be able to go beyond a certain level. Take Nizam-ud-Deen Awliya (RA) (a later Chishti, d. 1325) for example, we know that a lot of Hindus used to attend his gatherings, both the sermons and the *zikr*, and he

never turned them away because a Sufi believes that others will automatically start following him out of love.

Inayat Sahib has his roots in Silsila Chishtiya from the subcontinent and we respect that."

Private correspondence with several followers of Inayat Khan indicate that he did in fact prescribe the Muslim life for those wishing to make the most progress, but, not wishing to alienate most Western followers, has not publicized this nor made it mandatory. In recent times, Pir Zia Inayat Khan (1971-), present head of the Inayati, seems to live a Muslim lifestyle.

The symbol for Hazrat Inayat Khan's Sufi organization in the West is a winged red heart with the Islamic star and crescent moon in the middle of the heart. Since Islam literally means submission, the esoteric meaning of this beautiful design is, "The surrendered heart grows wings." However, the present day Inayati organization in Europe, The Sufi Movement (www.sufi-movement.org), describes this very same symbol in the following manner:

"The Sufi emblem is an illustration of several esoteric concepts related to the Religion of the Heart. The main symbol in the emblem suggests a mystical attunement to the heart as a divine temple within. The two wings illustrate the flight of the heart ascending toward higher spheres, where human love and divine love meet across the threshold of self-denial. The crescent moon, in its waxing and waning play with light, presents an inspiring picture of the heart's artful ability to offer unconditionally as well as to receive in humility and appreciation. The five pointed star, among the oldest symbols of guidance, is seen in the emblem as a reminder of the bright light within, which guides the longing heart, all along the journey toward its divine destination."

Note the absence of any mention of Islam. Indeed, a detailed search of this website fails to mention either Islam or the Chishti Order.

There is a later chapter which details the history of the creation of the Inayati order in the

West. It also discusses the roots of Sufism Re-oriented.

* * *

In recent years, perhaps due to sectarian and religious conflict in the Mideast, or in response to anti-sufi sentiments, several prominent Sufi Orders have made efforts to expand in the Western world.

The Shia Nimatullahi Order has thirteen or more centers in North America, nearly that many in Europe, Australia and Africa.

The Shadhili Order has several Western branches, each with multiple centers. This Sunni order, while their websites and literature pay due homage to the order's Islamic roots, does not in fact require conversion to Islam (*shahada*) when accepting an initiate murid (*bayat*).

There are some Muslim orders with Shaikhs who reportedly do not require a conversion to Islam: Sherif Chatalkaya ar-Rifa'I (Rifai Order); Khalid Bentounes al-Alawi (al-Alawi

Order); Farihah al-Jerrahi (Halveti Jerrahi Order).

IDRIES SHAH

Idries Shah (1924 - 1996) was a tireless writer and promoter of Sufism. His writings provide some of the most accessible information on the historical Sufi world. He also proved to be a most controversial character. Claims were made that he was the *MaShaikh*, the living head of the Naqshbandi Order in Afghanistan and the world.

Counterclaims posited that he learned most of his Sufism from libraries, and that he started writing about Sufism only after a series of trips to the MidEast in the 1950's.

His monumental work *The Sufis* published in 1964 is a thought-provoking look at Sufism throughout the ages. He admits, as hardcore Muslims may not, that there have always been Sufis, beings living as to invite God into their hearts. He breaks down some alleged Sufi secrets, such as decoding some Arabic triliteral roots, and discussing the numerical ABJAD system. On the other hand, the book stretches credulity when he claims that every part of western civilization owes its existence to hidden or apparent Sufi order activities.

Shah peppers his writings with quotations from many famous Sufis and was especially fond of relating stories about Mullah Nasruddin.

When his publisher and estate were queried regarding using short, attributed quotations from various Shah books for this book, they threatened legal action. I pointed out in vain that Shah had built his own writing career quoting long dead Sufi personages, people without the advantages of international copyright laws and aggressive solicitors.

G.I. GURDJIEFF

Georges I. Gurdjieff (1866/77? - 1949) was a Greek Armenian with a vast curiosity for the mystic. He formed a small group of like-minded travellers, and in the years prior to WWI, combed the Middle East for traces of real spirituality. The only history of his early life comes from his own writing. He attracted intellectuals as followers from Russia, Europe, and the U.K. He established working centers in France, Britain, and the USA.

A book, *Teachers Of Gurdjieff*, by Rafael LeFort, published 1966, purported to follow clues around the Middle East found in various Gurdjieff writings. These clues seemed to indicate Gurdjieff had been, among other things, a *murid* in various Sufi orders, primarily the Naqshbandi. He also mentions a possibly-apocryphal brotherhood deep in Afghanistan called the *Sarmoung*. However, this book is considered by some to have been written by Idries Shah and his brother Omar Ali-Shah in an effort to draw Gurdjieff followers to their own organization.

SUFIS WITHOUT ORDER

In the nineteenth and twentieth centuries there appeared in India several prominent spiritual persons with visible Muslim backgrounds, but who apparently achieved their status without rising through the ranks of any Sufi order.

The most famous of these was Sai Baba of Shirdi, Maharastra State (1838 est. - 1918). He remains possibly the best-known of all modern Indian Perfect Masters. He taught a mixture of Hindu and Muslim elements, and this was reflected in his devotees. He practiced the *salat*, the Muslim prayers, lived in a mosque, yet gave it the Hindu name *Dwarakamayi*. Sai was a master with a sense of humor. In the book 'The God-Man,' Charles Purdom wrote,

> "When Sai Baba wanted to move his bowels, people would take him in a procession with a band and pipes."

Sai's mix of Muslim and Hindu devotees is reminiscent of Hazrat Moinuddin Chishti's approach to spirituality, where followers of all religions were welcomed. Sai never claimed to be initiated in any of India's many Sufi *tariqas* or orders. However, Meher Baba said of Sai that Sai's actual spiritual mentor was the famous Chishti master, Zar Zari Zar Baksh, a *Qutb* of his age, buried in Maharastra State's Valley of the Saints, and who died 700 years before Sai's birth.

Other remarkable Indian saints of the late nineteenth and early twentieth centuries were Tajuddin Baba of Nagpur (1861-1925) and the prominent female Perfect Master Hazrat Babajan of Pune (1806 est. - 1931). Both these had Muslim backgrounds, yet there are no claimed or traceable antecedents for either as a *murid* or *murshid* of any known Sufi Order.

Professor Talat Halman (Central Michigan University) has equated these undeniably high yet unaffiliated beings with the Arabic term *Al-Afrad*, or *Fard*, the 'solitaries.' Murshid F.A. Ali Al-Senossi has written,

"These men (sic) are outside the supervision of the *Qutb*, or Pole. Their head is the Green Prophet, Al-Khidr."

In his website almirajsuficentre.org.au this term *Fard* is further defined:

"(*Fard/ Mufrad*). Within the Sufi hierarchy he is the man called *fard* (or mufrad) 'The Solitary'. He stands equal to the Pole (*Qutb*), but without a specific function such as that possessed by the Pole. He is the one who knows that he undergoes constant fluctuation of knowledge in each breath. He is outside the supervision of the qutb. He is compared to the 'Enraptured Angels' (*al mala'ikat al muhayyamin*)."

Among the Sleeping

PRESENT DAY MUSLIM SUFI ORDERS

Mevlevi Order

One Sufi organization very visible to the world is the Whirling Dervishes of Turkey. 'Dervish' is another word for Sufi. These Dervishes belong to the Mevlevi Order, begun in Konya in the thirteenth Century A.D. by one of the most famous of Sufis, a writer and poet named Mevlana (sometimes 'Maulana') Jellaludin Rumi. His most famous work is the *Mathnavi*, a book of intense spiritual insight. Rumi himself had a teacher, Shams of Tabriz (the 'sun' of Tabriz, in Iran), who was the *Qutb*, or spiritual axis, of his time. The divine knowledge, or gnosis, that Shams possessed was evidently greater than all of Rumi's formal study; Rumi abandoned his many students, gave up his books and became Sham's favorite disciple.

Rumi subsequently poured forth an ocean of poetry, including one of the most magnificent works in the Persian language, the 44,000 verse 'Divan of Shams Tabriz'.

Shams, it is said, had begged Allah for higher consciousness. "What will you give?" Allah said. Shams replied, "My head." Shams is quoted as saying,

> "It needs cycles after cycles for just one advanced soul to realize God."

This statement seems to support the concept of reincarnation, *hulul*, in discussing how long personal evolution can take. Or, it may be referring to making thousands of *rakats*, prostrations, while praying. Rumi seems to agree with reincarnation in this quatrain, or he may be talking about something else entirely:

> "Life is ending? God gives another. Admit the finite. Praise the infinite. Love is a spring. Submerge. Every separate drop, a new life."

Islam does not recognize reincarnation. Here is a situation where people with spiritual insight may be speaking in code, because reincarnation goes beyond the world of the Qur'an and *hadith* of the Prophet.

After some years with Rumi, Shams disappeared. It is rumored he was killed and beheaded by a jealous faction of Rumi's disciples.

If Shams was indeed the ranking spiritual personage incarnate on Earth at the time, how could this faction of young, hotheaded students-of-Rumi sneak up on him, abduct and murder him? Does not spiritual status confer a certain set of perceptions? If it does, then this becomes a deliberate martyrdom, 'suicide by *murid.*' Why? The answer may be in the next paragraph. Rumi needed his heart broken in order to begin the *Sama.*

After Shams' death, Rumi introduced a new teaching method. The Dervish Dancing used by the Mevlevi Order is called *Sama*, or audition, and is a moving meditation in which the music, each dancer's energy and movement, and the guidance of the Murshid combine into a vehicle for transcending ordinary consciousness.

A further note on the detachment of the Sufi. According to multiple histories, when Mevlana Rumi returned to teach his followers using the *Sama*, those followers included the very same group of young men who allegedly had murdered his master Shams. Consider the detachment necessary to continue to teach these spiritual aspirants.

Much classical Turkish music was developed over the centuries as part of the Dervish dancing ritual. During Rumi's lifetime he hosted gatherings including his own mystical poetry, *zikr*, music, and ecstatic movement and turning. His son, Sultan Veled, and grandson, Arif Chelebi, contributed poetry and further development and dissemination of the Mevlevi ritual in the form of Dervish dancing.

Qadiri Order

The Qadiri Sufi Order, branches of which are found throughout the Muslim world, was named after 'Abd al-Qadir Gilani, who died in Baghdad in the year 1166. Found from Morocco to India, the Qadiri Order is quite active in the modern era.

Abd al-Qadir Gilani is known as Ghaus Pak, or Ghaus-i-Azam, the Greatest Ghaus. The word *ghaus* has several meanings. Literally, it means one to whom we can cry for help. It also is one of the types of *Qutb*, or spiritual axis. Lastly, a *ghaus* type of mystic is one who dismembers his body's arms and legs. The body literally falls apart in praise of Allah, only to be miraculously reunited, in a process related to the Christian stigmata. (Sai Baba of Shirdi, d. 1918, was reputed to have this characteristic.) As a sober jurist, it is unlikely that Gilani was this last type of mystic.

As a young man, 'Abd al-Qadir became an eminent Islamic jurist of the Hanbali school, and had connections to other respected Islamic scholars including Imam Abu Hanifa. But instead of continuing as an scholar, he wandered

Iraq's deserts for twenty-five years as a disciple of various saints. He settled in Baghdad after the age of fifty, following a reported encounter and encouragement from the Green Saint, al-Khidr.

His clarity of thought, impressive oratory and many reputed miracles brought an enormous following, which soon coalesced into the Qadiri Order. He became known as the Rose of Baghdad. He is quoted as making this remarkable statement:

> "I have placed my foot upon the necks of all the saints."

He wrote some of the most influential books on Sufi mysticism, including *The Book Of The Secret Of Secrets And The Manifestation Of Lights* and *Revelations Of The Unseen*, and, especially revered on the subcontinent, *Sufficient Provision For Seekers Of The Path Of The Truth*. His *murids* included Shihabuddin Suhrawardi and Moinuddin Chishti.

Hazrat ('the Presence') 'Abd al-Qadir Gilani is honored by Sufis worldwide as the greatest *Ghaus* and *Qutb*, the center of the hierarchy of Saints around whom the world revolves, behind only the Prophet Muhammad and Caliph Ali.

Chishti Order

The Chishti Order is prevalent in Pakistan and India. The founder of the order was Shaykh Abu Ishaq Shami Chishti (d.940). In the modern era, the most famous Chishti is Hazrat ('the Presence') Khwaja ('the Master') Moinuddin Chishti (1141-1236). As a young man, Moinuddin Chishti met Qutb Abd al-Qadir Gilani in Baghdad in 1156.

While formalist Islam discouraged music because of its ability to rouse the carnal soul, it is said that Ghaus-i-Azam told Moinuddin Chishti,

"For you, music is permitted."

After travelling extensively, contacting the main Sufi masters of his age, and performing two Hajj, or pilgrimages to Mecca, his master, Hazrat Khwaja Usman Harooni (1096 est.-1220), sent Moinuddin to India to determine its suitability for the Sufi Work. He reached Ajmer, India, in 1191. A characteristic that has come down to us was Khwaja Moinuddin Chishti's sweet, approachable and forgiving nature. An interesting anomaly among Muslim saints, women are allowed full access to Chishti's *dargah* (tomb- shrine) in Ajmer.

Like the Mevlevis, the Chishti Order utilizes *Sama* sessions, with the addition of vocal and instrumental music called *qawwali*; the performers are called *qawwal*. During the *Sama* sessions, the Murshid may choose to assist the dancing participants to achieve the *hal* state, losing normal consciousness, later reporting seeing angels, saints, or the Prophet Muhammad, and drinking from Tasnim, the Well of Paradise. The Murshid instructs the Qawwali performers to keep playing the single phrase they were on when the dancers achieved *hal*; at that time the music is the soul's only link to this life. There are stories of *Sama* sessions where the *qawwali* singers were exhausted, and stopped singing and playing, and those in the *hal* state died.

While there are few or none authenticated statements direct from Khwaja, his successors have created a body of work they call 'Hazrat Khwaja's Message.' The Message includes these statements, which seem to imply that the Dervish or renunciate state is prefatory to that of the mystic, or advanced Sufi:

There are ten things necessary for a Dervish, namely, search of God, search of spiritual teacher, respect, surrender, love, piety, constancy and perseverance, to eat less, to sleep less, seclusion, and last of all, prayers and fasting.

For the mystic, also, there are likewise, 10 things necessary:

1. to be perfect in Divine knowledge

2. to be neither sorry and sad himself nor to make others sorry and sad, and not to think evil of anybody

3. to point the way towards God, and to lead and guide the people towards the Ultimate Good

4. to be hospitable; to prefer seclusion

5. to pay respect and regard to every one, and to count himself as the humblest and the lowest

6. to surrender his will to the Will of God

7. to be patient and persevering in every grief and woe;

8. to be humble and meek

9. to be contented

10. to repose his trust in God

Suhrawardi Order

Diya ad-din Abu 'n-Najib as-Suhrawardi (d.1168) left Suhraward in Persia as a young man and became an initiate of al-Ghazzali in Baghdad. He later built a center on a ruined site along the river Tigris. He wrote *Kitab Adab al-Muridin, A Sufi Rule for Novices,* which describes the proper *adab* (manner) and attitudes for murids joining a Sufi *khanqah*, or center. This book has been used for centuries as part of the teaching in many orders. Abu 'n- Najib attracted many *murids* who later became prominent Sufis. Chief among them was his nephew Shihabuddin Abu Hafs Umar (d.1234), who is regarded as the founder of the Suhrawardiyya.

Shihabuddin maintained a careful Muslim orthodoxy, wrote an influential book, *Awarif al-ma'arif, Knowledge for Encountering God,* and was known as a great teaching-*shaikh*. Because of his habit of granting the Khalifa's *khirqa* to many aspirants, the Suhrawardi Order spread far and wide, with a great number of Sufis throughout the centuries claiming to belong to the Order.

Uwaisi Order

The Uwaisi Order of Sufis is unique. Like a river in the desert which may go underground for long stretches, the Uwaisi Order appears in history for a period, then disappears and reappears. Its founder, a Yemeni named Uwais al-Qarani (594-657), was a contemporary of Prophet Muhammad, yet they never met. Merely hearing of the Prophet was enough to create a strong connection — *tawaj, rab'ta, tassawur-I-Rasul* — between the two men. Once Uwais heard that Muhammad had lost two teeth in a battle, he broke his own in response.

According to tradition Uwais was visited by the Prophet in a vision and was granted a *Darood*, a phrase to be meditated upon and recited, much like *zikr*. Uwais was unable to ever meet the Prophet. His followers consider that they are rightly guided by Uwais, similar to the occasional reports of those without a teacher being contacted by al-Khidr.

As Uwais was totally absorbed into the Light of the Prophet, *nur-I-Muhammad*, his followers consider the Prophet to be the still loving and living link to Allah.

The Uwaisi Darood

Bismillah ar-Rahman ar-Rahim
In the name of the Compassionate, the Merciful (God)

Allahumma salay ala Sayeddina
We request God to send peace and salutations

Wa maulana Ya Muhammado
Upon our Guide Muhammad

Nin na beeyul Ummi yo
Who is unlettered (Ummi), (beyond all styles)

Wa alaihi wasalaam
And unto the followers, Peace

Malamatis and Qalandars

There are loose organizations of spiritual seekers in the East called the *Malamati*, or blameworthy ones. These people conceal their spiritual aspirations, and if they do have a murshid, that person is likely to be hidden – *mastur*.

Tradition states there have only been two and a half real Qalandars that walked the earth. The original Qalandar Bu-Ali Shah Qalandar (1299-1324), Lal Shahbazz Qalandar (1149-1179), and the already mentioned Rabia al-Adawiyya / al-Basri (714 est.-801), who was 'half Qalandar.' Qalandars closely resemble Malamatis in their disregard for Islamic sensibilities. The word Qalandar may be from the Persian for 'coarse one.' These people have few possessions and travel incessantly. They act as if they are outside the *Sharia*, in order to be condemned by the Muslim society around them. The Qalandar believes that they earn spiritual benefits from voluntarily attracting condemnation and attendant exclusion from Muslim society.

There is even an Order in Pakistan, the Qalandariyya, whose *Silsila* includes the First

Three: Bu-Ali Shah, Lal Shahbazz Qalandar, and Rabia al-Basri. This is considered a very intense *Jelali* Order.

NAQSHBANDI ORDER

Naqshbandi Dervishes can be found from Morocco to Indonesia. Oddly, the order existed long before it gained its current name. The Khwajagan (Masters) were well known for their exercise *habs-i-dam*, or restraint of breath, and by their use of silent *zikr, wazifa*. The order received its later name from Muhammad Bahauddin who died in 1390. Bahauddin, originally of Bokhara, spent seven years as a courtier, seven looking after animals, and seven in road building, before he became a teaching master.

Someone said to Bahauddin Naqshband, "It must have caused you pain to dismiss a certain student." He said:

> "The best of all ways to test and help a disciple, it if is possible, may be to dismiss him. If he then turns against you, he has a chance of observing his own shallowness and the defects which led to the dismissal. If he forgives you, he has an opportunity of seeing whether in that there is any sanctimoniousness. If he regains his balance, he will be able to bene-

fit the Teaching, and especially to benefit himself."

What made Bahauddin assume the surname Naqshband? The word *naqsh* means a seal, or a symbol, or sign. Another meaning of *naqsh* is print or impression, and band is to bind, or fasten. Naqshbandis practice the silent *zikr*, *wazifa*, which is therefore imprinted upon the heart. The Naqshbandis are also known as the Builders or Designers.

OTHER PROMINENT ORDERS

Rifai, Khalwati, Kubravi, Hanafi, Bektashi, Hamadani, Yasavi, Badawi

Sci-Fi Sufis

In the twentieth century, several well regarded authors wrote science fiction novels examining the concept of the perfectibility of man. Robert Heinlein wrote several books examining this concept, the best of which was *Stranger in a Strange Land.*

The protagonist was Valentine Michael Smith, the son of the first scientists to crash on Mars. The next Mars mission was twenty years later, and Smith was discovered, alive, speaking no English, having been raised by Martians. Brought back to Earth, the ultimate innocent, he was a pawn in a political game, because, according to international law, he owned Mars. However, the people with whom he stayed discovered that he could commit miracles at will, by simply thinking in Martian.

Smith began teaching Martian to his close companions, wanting to help mankind to rise, but finding that most applicants had little aptitude for learning Martian. He continued gaining power and influence, spreading his knowledge, and his companions learned to perform minor miracles. This came to the attention of the political and religious authorities, who repeatedly tried to close down various offshoots of his organization.

The novel ends with him voluntarily presenting himself for martyrdom, blessing those who kill him, and ultimately transcending death.

By any standard, *Stranger in a Strange Land* is a remarkable book, even more so if looked at as a metaphor for Sufi development; speaking a new language with new concepts, which only a few are prepared to handle, bringing new perceptual abilities and empathy to man.

Time, Place, and People

There is a Sufi phrase, *Zaman, Makan, Ikhwan*, which is a shorthand recognition that in order for transformation to take place, a certain confluence of conditions must exist — enough of the right kind of time, *zaman*, the right place(s), *makan*, and especially the right, and rightly guided, people, *ikhwan*.

In Conclusion

According to Shaqiq of Balkh (d.810), among the characteristics of a genuine Sufi are: "First, freedom from anxiety for one's daily sustenance; second, sincerity of action and a pure heart."

Shaqiq's own resolve to enter the path was triggered during a great famine in Balkh, when he observed a slave who went about without the least worry. Shaqiq asked him, "Aren't you worried about the famine?"

"My master has a lot of grain," the slave replied.

SUFISM AND JIHADISTS

Anyone who has heard the news in the past thirty years may have a difficult time reconciling the story of the Sufis and the story of the Jihadists. There is a photo in the July 4, 2005 *Time Magazine*, a closeup of someone holding a Quran and a grenade. While the photo may have been posed, it begs the question - how does one get from the Qur'an to a grenade?

There is no simple answer. Superficial study of Arabian history presents a simple chain of cause and effect. This is how one argument goes:

A History

Portions of the Arabian peninsula, mostly northeast and central, were under Ottoman – Turkish – control for hundreds of years. The native inhabitants were Bedouin nomads whose wealth was in camels and raiding or extorting from the caravan trade, and townspeople, whose villages or towns were mostly waystations for those caravans.

In 1703, Muhammad ibn Abdul Wahhab was born in Nejd. (d.1792). He was trained as a jurist, and gained quite a following over time, preaching that Islam had to return to its origins, that all alien, non-Islamic beliefs, such as *ziyarat*, or tomb-visits, or even exaggerated respect for the Prophet, was essentially *shirk*, (placing anything on a level with Allah) and thus must be cleansed. They were and are vehemently opposed to Sufis, whose practices he decried as *bidaa*, an unwelcome innovation not in place at the time of the Prophet.

Calling this group 'Wahhabi' is a bit of a misnomer, in that its central tenet is *tawheed*, the Oneness of Allah—they might rightly be called Unitarians or Muwahhidun. Yet, in modern usage 'Wahhabi' refers to these people and to the strict interpretations they make of Islamic law.

In 1744 Abdul ibn Wahhab met Muhammad ibn Saud (d. 1765), ruler of the town of Dar'iyah, near the present day capital of Riyadh. Ibn Wahhab became the religious leader of

Dar'iyah, and thus began the long partnership between the Wahhabi and the tribe led by the house of Saud. The division of duties seemed to be that secular authority belonged to the Saudis, and the Wahhabi had the religious authority.

The Saudis began moving outward, attacking Riyadh and neighboring towns. In 1802, they conquered Mecca, Medina and Taif, the three most important towns in Islam, the goals of the *Hajj* pilgrimage. Since Taif resisted, ibn Wahhab's grandson decreed all of Taif's adult males should be slaughtered. Shrines and idols in both Mecca and Medina were smashed, and when pilgrims from Egypt and Syria arrived the army turned them away as idolaters.

The Prophet Muhammad had made a clear distinction between the 'greater' *Jihad*, or struggle with one's own tendencies, or *nafs*, and the 'lesser' *Jihad*, the armed struggle for survival, or dominion over lands and people. The Wahhabi sacking of Mecca and Medina, and their entire approach to religious purity demonstrates an exaggerated notion of Tawheed, or the oneness of God, along with a gross misinterpretation of the concept of 'lesser' *Jihad*.

Since the Turks had retreated, for a time Arabia was united under the Saudis. However, this was not to last. The Ottomans, with modern firepower, re-took the Hejaz, the eastern part of the country, encompassing Mecca, Medina, and Taif. The Saudis, under the famous Abdul Aziz ibn Saud, didn't regain the Meccan region until 1902.

The Turks returned in the opening days of WWI, only to be driven back forever by Abdul Aziz' warriors, armed to a degree by Britain. Britain promised Abdul Aziz that the northern territory, now known as Syria and Iraq, would be annexed to the Saudis in exchange for their help in expelling the Ottomans. See T.E. Lawrence's (1888-1935) *Seven Pillars of Wisdom* for a detailed look at the shell game played by France and Britain.

Despite these setbacks, by 1920 the Saudi family was in firm control of the Arabian peninsula. Poor as their Bedouin, they had a hard time as a nation until the extent of their oilfields was discovered in the early 1930's. The nascent petroleum industry had barely gotten a start in Arabia when it was interrupted by WWII.

After WWII, an energy-hungry world turned to Saudi Arabia once again. Partnerships were struck with British, American, and Dutch oil companies. Petrodollars began flowing into this country of 4 million inhabitants. Wahhabis controlled the policies of key ministries including Education and Justice. Ibn Wahhab's legal interpretations and judgements of Islamic practice pervade the Saudi legal system. Wahhabis comprise the religious police forces in Saudi Arabia, looking for infractions, and police the millions of pilgrims coming annually to *Hajj*.

Present Day

Within the borders of Saudi Arabia, continuing their policies from the mid-1800's, Wahhabis have relentlessly sought to minimize the possibility of a cult of personality around the Prophet Muhammad. Paranoid about *Hajj* pilgrims' visits to places associated with the Prophet, they have destroyed every site possible – flattening graveyards outside Mecca and Medina where companions of the Prophet are buried, threatening the house where the Prophet was born, planning a shopping mall. Other than the Kaaba in Mecca and the Prophet's grave in

Medina, the remaining holy sites of Islam are mostly outside the borders of Saudi Arabia.

After the fall of the Shah of Iran in 1979, the Saudi Ministry of Education began to export its flavor of Islam, possibly to counteract Iran's Shia message. Wahhabi-trained *Imams* were sent on missions to Western countries, where, using Saudi petrodollars, they began construction of mosques and *madrassas* – Muslim schools. In recent years the Education Ministry has redoubled its efforts. There are thousands of these institutions in the West – Europe, Britain, and the USA, representing billions (some estimates say over $80B) of Saudi money, plus donations from Muslims worldwide to Islamic charities who may or may not be funnelling money into arms purchases or radical *madrassas*.

One of the painful paradoxes is that Western oil money may in many cases be directly be traced to financing training of West-hating Jihadists. There are many Western and Islamic observers who consider the Wahhabi teachings in these *madrassas* to be instrumental in radicalizing young Muslims, even those born far from Saudi Arabia.

However, like all generalizations, this one is not universally applicable.

Saudi-funded *madrassas* never made any inroad into Muslim education in Afghanistan or Pakistan. Instead, a shadowy international group known as the Muslim Brotherhood has funded hundreds of *madrassas* where Islamic education is even more repressive than ibn Wahhab's. While they eschew any practical education, concentrating on Qur'anic studies, many of these Afghan and Pakistani *madrassas* easily morphed straight into arms training and bomb building. A *talib* is a student. The *Taliban*, trained in armed *madrassa* camps, became the army that evicted the Soviet Union from Afghanistan. The ultrafundamentalist regime they subsequently created should have been a surprise to no one. This extends to their harboring al-Qaeda in remote areas even after the US invasion.

The 'Wahhabi/Saudi money creates Jihadists' explanation above also does not address the existence of Shi'ite terrorists. Unlikely to pay attention to a Saudi/Wahhabi/Sunni educational model, Iran has developed their own particular hardline Islamism since their revolution, and there have been Shi'ite anti-Sufi riots in various cities in Iran, traditionally quite tolerant of Sufi activities.

In addition, one must not apply religious motives when they are actually secular. Iraq is a case in point. As a country with three disparate populations, it would have never existed as a nation without the Balfour Declaration and domination by Britain and France after WWI. It took the brutal hand of the Baathists and then Saddam Hussein to keep the country under control. Iraq remained a civil war waiting to happen. Following the departure of US 'peacekeeping' forces, armed Shi'ite and Sunni militias simply struggled for influence and territory.

There are commonalities in all of the hard-line, armed groups.

Jihadist groups are comprised of young persons with indifferent education and worse prospects, from countries with little or no industrial base. These are people with no future. This does not explain wealthy Saudi jihadists, admittedly, other than stating the obvious, that these have had a lifetime of Wahhabi Islamic education.

Many young Muslims are being taught a bizarre and involved mix of Western/Zionist conspiracy theories, claiming that there has been a 2-millennia-old Zionist conspiracy to keep the Muslims in their place, along the way quoting the long-debunked *Protocols of the Elders of Zion*, used by the National Socialists in Germany to justify their notions of racial purity. The theories are replete with names of Jewish financiers, and point fingers at the World Bank, the policies of the International Monetary Fund, and the United Nations.

The state of Israel is their proof that the world cares more for Zionists than Muslims, and since the friend of my enemy is my enemy, all countries with trade or diplomatic relations with Israel may be considered fair game.

Jihadists have been taught a strict interpretation of Islamic jurisprudence where killing infidels is the fastest road to heaven. They envision a global Islamic state with no alcohol, no music, and no Western influence. The Jihadist will point to the Qur'anic Sura Al-Anfal, or *The Spoils of War.*

"Against them make ready your strength to the utmost of your power, including steeds of war, to strike terror into the enemy of Allah and your enemy." 8:60

Jihadists have also seen that armed struggle and bombing, while it may not bring them power, at least keeps entire regions unsettled, and, as in Iraq, after the USA left, they might be better positioned to take control. The group ISIS is simply a loose coalition of Sunni militias, operating freely across borders.

Characterizing Muslim mindsets is necessarily an anecdotal process. In my experience, even moderate young Muslims have a combination of a huge inferiority complex coupled with religious grandiosity. They often believe Jews (controlling international finance) and the USA are keeping them down. Based on the interpretations of Islam they have been taught, some radicals obviously believe it is legal and even mandated that they attempt to kill the oppressors, especially if those are *kaffirs* or unbelievers – ignoring that the Qur'an refers to Jews and Christians and Muslims alike as 'people of the Book' and fellow believers in the one God.

Pointing at European colonialism as the root of their troubles, radical and moderate Muslims alike ignore centuries of brutal, ineffective and corrupt Islamic regimes and rulers, long-existing tribal schisms, and ongoing Sunni – Shia politico-military struggles. Muslims, despite all the rhetoric, have rarely acted as brothers in unity. One could fairly say that economic colonialism is still being practiced. Other than oil, few Muslim nations have anything the West desires. However, in a worldwide oil-based energy market, control of and access to oil drives a myriad of behaviors, Mid-East and Western.

It is fair to say that Jihadists and Sufis represent the two extremes of Muslim life. It is quite difficult to reconcile these two fruits of the Islamic tree – one dedicated to destruction in the world, hoping for an Islamic future, or at least martyrdom leading to Paradise, the other dedicated to bringing out the latent higher capabilities within mankind.

CAST OF CHARACTERS

Murshida Rabia Martin

Hazrat Inayat Khan

Abu Hashim Madani

Pir Zia Inayat Khan

Vilayat Khan

Hazrat Inayat Khan

The Royal Musicians of Hindustan circa 1910: Ali Khan, Inayat Khan, Musheraff Khan and Maheboob Khan

Samuel Lewis

Hasan Nizami

Ijaza Nama

SUCCESSION

Murshida Rabia Martin and the passing of Hazrat Inayat Khan

In 1910, under orders from his Murshid, the Indian Chishti musician Hazrat Inayat Khan sailed to America to spread the message of Sufism in the West. He encountered Mrs. Ada Martin in San Francisco, who became his first Western *murid*, and who was trained by him as a Murshida. Khan spent most of the next sixteen years in Europe and England, where he founded a dozen or more spiritual centers. After his sudden death in India in 1927, there was a three-year struggle within Khan's organization, mostly regarding the legitimacy of Murshida Martin's claim that she had been appointed Inayat Khan's spiritual successor in the West. She was ultimately rejected.

She and her *murids* then spent another thirteen years in relative isolation in America, until Martin discovered the existence of Meher Baba in the early 1940s. She became convinced he was the ranking spiritual leader of this age, corresponded heavily with him, and offered the control of her two spiritual groups in California to Meher Baba. In 1952, several years after Martin's death, Meher Baba, Martin's successor Ivy O. Duce and *murid* Don Stevens created the charter of Sufism Reoriented. This oriented Martin's groups toward Meher Baba, not the Prophet Muhammad, as the Perfect Man.

NEW INFORMATION

When considering the roots of the Sufism Reoriented movement, I have heard and read that the reason Murshida Rabia Martin was denied her proper place as the inheritor of Hazrat Inayat Khan's mantle was the prejudice of the Indian Muslim brothers and cousins of Inayat Khan. It is claimed they denied Martin because she was American, a woman, and a Jew. Add the apparent absurdity of claiming that Inayat's son Vilayat, all of eleven years old at Inayat's death, was an initiated *Khalif*, and the case for Martin and against those prejudiced

Muslim males seems complete. Knowing the period, and the deeply held beliefs of Muslims, even advanced Sufis, this explanation seems to hold up over time. Take also in account that at the time of his passing in 1927 women in America had the right to vote for only seven years. A Jewish female head of a Sufi order in America shows Khan's incredibly advanced attitude, which his male, Muslim relatives might not have shared.

This chapter will attempt to make Khan's Sufi Order's rejection of Murshida Martin more understandable, using sources including letters from Meher Baba, articles from Sufism Reoriented, and finally a very interesting source, Inayat Khan's grandson Pir Zia Inayat Khan, the head of the present-day Sufi Order International and Sufi Movement. Pir Zia's 377-page doctoral dissertation, presented at Duke University in 2006 towards a Ph.D in religion, is titled *A Hybrid Sufi Order at the Crossroads of Modernity: the Sufi Order and Sufi Movement of Pir-o-Murshid Inayat Khan*, and is the history of Inayat Khan's life and carries the story up to the present day. I feel it is a valuable document, a view from the inside, so to speak. It draws upon archives in India, Europe and the United

States, and, most interesting to me, on the archives of Sufism Reoriented in Walnut Creek. A primary source for Pir Zia was the voluminous correspondence between Inayat Khan and Rabia Martin.

The dissertation begins with a brief history of the Chishti Order in India, then veers away to European spirituality including the Theosophical movement and Madame Blatavsky (1831-1891), and the phenomenon of Swami Vivekenanda (1863-1902).

Inayat Khan's Early Days

Inayat Khan's musical development began early, being born into an accomplished musical family accustomed to playing for luminaries such as the Nizam of Hyderabad (1886-1911). Inayat's instrument was the *vina*, a stringed instrument played similarly to a sitar. His singing and playing placed him high in the musical hierarchy of Baroda.

Inayat was initiated and trained in the four Indian *tariqas* or Sufi Orders - Chishti, Naqshbandi, Suhrawardi, and Qadiri. Abu Hashim Madani, his own Murshid, also initiated into multiple Orders, presented himself and trained his *murids* as a Chishti.

Within the Western Sufi organizations he founded, Inayat's story was construed to have distanced him from a pure Chishti or Islamic tradition. A biographical essay published by the Sufi Movement in 1964 contends:

> "Although his own Murshid and initiator (Madani) belonged to the Chishtiyya order of Sufis, Hazrat Inayat Khan *cannot, strictly speaking, be considered as a link between Chishti teaching and the West*, for neither his origin nor his education, culture, or esoteric training should obscure the fact that the essence of the Sufism he taught is the *product of his individual achievement and originality.*" (italics mine.)

A few years ago the website of the European Sufi Movement had a detailed description of the heart-with-wings emblem adopted quite early by Inayat Khan. This emblem depicted a crescent moon and star (symbolic of Islam, or surrender) within a winged heart. The esoteric meaning is 'the surrendered heart grows wings.' The description on the website omitted any mention of Islam or even the Chishti Order.

Pir Zia's dissertation states the young Inayat, already a world-class musician, was given an 'injunction' by his Chishti Murshid, Sayyid Abu Hashim Madani of Hyderabad (d. 1910). Madani granted Inayat a certificate of succession, known as an *ijazat nama* or *khilafat-nama* in 1907 and instructed him to travel to the West and disseminate the Sufi wisdom. However, Inayat did not depart for America for three more years, doing local pilgrimages and spending his time touring South India, Ceylon and Burma, recording music, and settling in Calcutta. The dissertation refers to a biography where Inayat's son and successor Vilayat wrote:

> "When the time of his passing was nigh, Khwaja (master) Madani made Inayat Khan his successor in the Chain of Sufis, saying he had received from Khwaja Muinuddin Chishti (founder of the Order in India, d. 1236) instructions to tell him he was missioned to carry the Sufi Message to the West."

Note the disparity here. In one case above we are told that Inayat is NOT to be construed as carrying the Chishti torch to the West, essentially, because of his strong individuality. Yet here is Inayat's own son Vilayat claiming the most traditionally Sufi injunction of all, a command from the founder of the Order in India and what is now Pakistan.

The West and Meeting Rabia Martin

After his father passed on in 1910, Inayat booked passage to New York with his brother Maheboob Khan and cousin Muhammad Ali Khan. This departure from India was later called Hejirat Day in the Sufi Movement and gives us an inkling of the stature of Inayat in the later Sufi view. This anniversary deliberately invokes the Prophet Muhammad's *hejira* from Mecca to Medina. It was also later termed "the birthday of the Message." A "prophetic resonance," as Pir Zia wrote.

Khan's musical troupe "The Royal Musicians of Hindustan" traveled with a famous dancer, Ruth St. Denis (1879-1968), across America to San Francisco. The group parted ways with St. Denis, as Inayat felt American audiences had, in that company, considered them mere entertainment.

Khan was soon invited to speak at San Francisco's Vedanta Temple, where Mrs. Ada Martin first heard him, on Easter Sunday afternoon April 16, 1911. She followed the group to their next concert. Pir Zia wrote, "Soon thereafter Inayat initiated her as his first murid, granted her the honorary name (*laqab*) Rabia, and began her training. This was the beginning of Inayat Khan's Sufi work..." In other words, the actual Work in the West began with this one person's recruitment. Pir Zia continued,

> "Several others were initiated in the wake of Martin, but she was to remain Inayat Khan's *primary student and prospective representative in America.*" (italics mine.)

Pir Zia's dissertation Chapter Three, "The Genesis of the Sufi Order, 1910-1920," is spent describing the circumstances of Rabia and Inayat's meeting and the development of her spirituality under his guidance-by-letter. It is also clear that by late 1911, Inayat already considered her the front-runner as his successor in

America. No other American *murids* are even mentioned in this chapter by Pir Zia, except Samuel Lewis (1896-1971), who appears only as a witness and sometime-secretary to Martin.

Pir Zia describes the intense exchange of letters between Rabia and Inayat, in which Inayat began instructing her in standard Chishti training, such as so many *zikr* (repetitions of the names of God) daily, watching the heart, etc. Pir Zia reports on Martin's progress in some detail:

> "By the end of 1911 Martin had received instructions in all of the basic practices. Inayat wrote (her), 'You have now to continue your practice of *wayalat* [*'amal*] with *Zikr*, *Fikr* (silent repetitions), *shagal* and *darood* forever.' The focus of his letters now shifted to the mission of establishing Sufism in America, and Martin's important role in this. From New York he wrote: '...I want somebody to undertake my mission as my successor in America before I would leave (for Europe) ... *I find you the most suited of my murids* ... All this shows that God almighty and all Murshids in Chain* have selected you to bestow

upon you this honour..." 'Chain' is a direct translation of the Arabic-Sufi term *silsila*, the Sufi succession back to 'Ali and the Prophet. (italics mine)

Pir Zia then states:

"...it is evident that ... Rabia Martin in particular received an intensive and systematic course of esoteric training that *differed little in form from the Sufism practiced among Chishti initiates in India.*" (italics mine.)

Inayat spent little time in California, and most of his subsequent years were in Britain and France, leaving Rabia and her group isolated, teaching a traditional Muslim Chishti spirituality; Inayat had instructed Rabia to learn Arabic and study the Qur'an.

BUILDING SUFISM IN BRITAIN AND EUROPE

Chapter Three then follows Inayat Khan to Britain in 1912, and gives a background for what Pir Zia terms "Occidental Sufism," and the formation of the Sufi Order In The West in London, 1917. He discusses the inherent contradictions of introducing Indian - Islamic Sufism into a "secular Christian milieu."

The influence of the West grew perceptibly on Inayat personally and on his methods of imparting the Message to the West. In 1913 Ora Ray Baker (1892-1949) arrived in London. She was a cousin of the founder in America of the Christian Science movement, Mary Baker Eddy (1821-1910). Ora Ray was dubbed 'Pirani Ameena Begum' (Female master, Knower, and Princess) by Inayat and they married that same year. Inayat began meeting well-regarded artists, musicians and royalty, and wrote to Rabia, "I have already started the Sufi movement in Paris and now I am going to spread it in England." A meeting with Claude Debussy (1862-1918) led to an invitation for his group, the Royal Musicians of Hindustan, to play in Russia, where Inayat "...lectured to large audiences and was widely introduced in musical circles."

During this period Inayat and his extended family lived in Addison Road in London. Brothers and cousin Maheboob, Mohammed Ali, Musharaff, and Inayat's new wife Ameena Begum were all trained intensively by Inayat, and were considered to be the core of the Sufi

Movement in England. This group was essentially stranded in London when WWI broke out, temporarily severing ties with groups in Europe and Russia. They moved to another London home in 1915, which was dubbed the *Khanaqah* (headquarters) of the Sufi Order. Two of Inayat's four children were born during the war, Vilayat in 1916, Hidayat in 1917, then Khair-un-nisa just afterward in 1919. A close riend of the family at that time, Gujarat native Abdullah Yusuf Ali, later gained fame in the Muslim world as a translator of the Qur'an.

However, the Western influence continued. Pir Zia notes that "beginning in 1915, 'God' began to replace 'Allah' in Inayat's articles [in *The Sufi*, their English periodical]," and "..as time progressed Islamic references consistently diminished in all of the Order's publications." In 1920 Inayat wrote to Rabia Martin:

> "... by experience I can work with the Western people much better than before. I have studied their psychology and I know what they like and what they do not like and how to approach them on these subjects and therefore I have been lately successful too."

One possible reason for the diminished role of Muslim terminology, Pir Zia proposes, was rising anti-Islamic sentiment among the English due to the failed Gallipoli campaign in 1915, shortly after the London *Khanaqah* was formed. Hostility toward the Turks extended to all things Islamic and was fanned by the press. Rabia and her group, isolated in America, were not exposed to this Westward slide of the Sufi movement.

During the war years Inayat spread the Order in the British Isles through lectures and appearances, sometimes hosted by various local Theosophical Society groups. Small lodges opened in Harrogate, Southampton, Tottenham (later home of the Who), Brighton, and Luton.

Pir Zia points out in the very next paragraph that Rabia Martin "... was making progress in San Francisco. In 1918 she opened a center on Sutter Street, and a second center, Kaaba Allah, in rural Marin County." In the dissertation, along with the history of Inayat Khan's travels and creation and dissolution of groups, Pir Zia never loses sight of Rabia Martin. He often indicates what's going on in

Inayat's mind by including excerpts from a massive volume of correspondence between them from 1911 to his death in 1927. Pir Zia gives more attention to Rabia Martin than any individual besides Inayat Khan himself. Inayat's regard for Rabia Martin is never downplayed by Pir Zia, neither overtly by editorializing nor covertly by omitting her from the narrative.

At the end of WWI in late 1918, Inayat and extended family incorporated the Sufi Trust Limited. The group had been appealing for a building to be used as a permanent *Khanaqah*, and a wealthy *murid* donated the lease on a "palatial property" at 29 Gordon Square in central London. This center soon dissolved due to financial disputes.

A Universal Church

Possibly in reaction, in 1919, Inayat moved his family to Tremblaye, France. He determined that the Sufi Order's new international headquarters should be established in Geneva. Pir Zia sees a connection between this move of the Sufis to Geneva and the transfer of the League of Nations from London to Geneva. Following the brutal and murderous War to End

All Wars, the League of Nations was then seen as the hope and promise of world peace.

Sufi Order membership in Britain and Europe grew slowly in this first decade. Pir Zia characterizes it as:

> "... the result of many factors. Muslims soon felt uncomfortable within the Order's quasi-religious but not specifically Islamic framework. Jews and Christians were sometimes ill at ease with the Order's hybrid mix of Theosophy and Islam. Theosophists were attracted by Inayat Khan's resemblance to the legendary oriental 'Masters' and piqued by the possibility that he might be the awaited 'World-Teacher,' but were, in many cases, disappointed to find he did not fit the mold of their expectations."

In letters to Rabia, Inayat recommended she delay legalizing the American branch of the Order. He wrote her from Geneva that he wished to return to America to help her "rebuild," but said he must first work on the affairs of the European branches.

In 1920 the Khan family moved to Wissous, France, and a Parisian Sufi group was formed. Khan visited Britain twice in 1921. One of the marked changes in this period was the creation of the Church of All. This heterodox organization showed the movement away from a Sufi esoteric tradition into a new religious movement, and the phrase "Universal Worship" was coined. Inayat created a class of officiants called *Cherags* (from the Persian for 'lamp'), and created certain prescribed rituals for services.

During this period there was more mention and awareness, within the various European Sufi groups, that Inayat Khan should be considered Messenger of the Age, seen on a level with the Prophet Muhammad. The remaining strict Muslims within the Order could point to verses in the Qur'an, 40:78, 10:48, 16:36, and 35:24, which seem to allow subsequent Messengers to mankind. Pir Zia states:

> "On the basis of this verse [40:78], the 18th century Naqshbandi shaykh Jan-i-Janan (1699-1781) wrote: 'When the holy Qur'an has preferred to remain silent about many prophets, it is incumbent on

us to adopt a liberal attitude with regard to the prophets of India.'"

Pir Zia also writes:

"In an unpublished compilation of personal narratives by 46 original murids titled *Memories of Murshid*, Inayat is variously referred to as the World-Teacher, Christ, Christ-man, Prophet, Messenger, Rabi, and Rasul."

Inayat Khan is alleged to have acknowledged these perceptions in private. Any Sufi order, regardless of founder or location, would say that its goal is to reproduce the heart-states of the Prophet Muhammad in the followers who are capable. Pir Zia continues reportage of the perceptions of Inayat's followers for several pages of Chapter Four. He points out that, since Inayat was a full Murshid, having undergone the complete Sufi training, beginning with *fana* (annihilation) into his master Madani (*fana fi-shaikh*), who transferred his consciousness to the Prophet Muhammad (*fana fi-Rasul*) who in turn handed him to God (*fana fi'llah*), then in a sense Inayat Khan was indeed one with the Prophet. However, this ignores the fact that any

Kamil Shaikh (perfected *murshid*) could claim the same state and status.

Inayat Khan returned to America in February 1923 intending a three month long tour. He remained in San Francisco for seven weeks, giving public lectures and private classes for murids. These lectures were edited and later published under the title *Gita Dhyana*.

Later that year Inayat traveled to Geneva, and began a revision of the Sufi charters. He merged the Sufi Order into the Sufi Movement, which included the Brotherhood and the Universal Worship. He handed the creation of the new constitution to Enrique Zanetti, a Harvard-trained lawyer. Inayat continued to Germany and Holland, where brother Maheboob Khan lived with his new bride, and on to Belgium. He continued travel through 1924, offering lectures across France, Switzerland, Italy, Germany, and England. New centers sprouted in his wake. His lectures were transcribed and transmitted to Geneva headquarters.

A new center was created in Suresnes, France. Several leaders and murids had homes or second homes in Suresnes. Earlier Inayat wrote Rabia that the little town "will become a Sufi colony"... and it did.

In Europe and England, as Pir Zia describes, Inayat created new levels of certification within the Esoteric School, giving four Circles of Initiation, each with three internal grades, and so on. He contrasts this with the comparatively simple structure of Orders in the East: the *bayat*, initiation of a *murid*, and *khilafat*, the movement to junior *murshid* status. Inayat had clearly moved the European organizations far away from the original Chishti model. These changes were notably absent in the groups led by Murshida Martin.

As the number of centers in multiple countries grew, there was an added bureaucratic level of administrators, all the way to the highest level within the Sufi Movement. Inayat Khan found himself simultaneously the Pir-o-Murshid of the Esoteric School, functioning as an Eastern-style spiritual master, endowed with the authority of *insan al-kamil* (perfect man), and also as the administrative head, the Representative General of the international Sufi Movement. In late 1925 at an annual council meeting at Geneva Headquarters, while Khan was traveling, a constitutional proposal was made to abolish the Representative General's vote in the Executive Committee, since that position held both four votes and the power of veto. Politics and voting. As Pir Zia puts it:

> "Did the Sufi Movement exist to serve the Pir-o-Murshid's agenda, or did the Pir-o-Murshid exist to serve the Movement's agenda?"

Essentially they were defining the difference between esoteric and exoteric authority. Some within the hierarchy of the Movement felt strongly that as Khan was the Messenger, that all such politics was destructive, since the Murshid was in a state of *fana fi-illah*, he essentially was the voice of God, infallible. Of course this attitude implies total dependence upon that individual. Others believed that Khan was so absorbed in the spiritual that he had neither time nor interest in the temporal, and used Khan's frequent absences from meetings as evidence. A response to that was "... a mystic is not dependent on what various people tell him." The result of this particular vote was ten in favor, seven against. When presented to Inayat Khan, he cast his four votes against, and the attempt to limit Khan's constitutional powers failed.

In a subsequent letter to his wife, he wrote, referring to the vote:

> "When a disciple begins to judge the teacher or his actions, to criticize his teachings, or try to test his inspiration or power, however cleverly he may do it, he ceases to be a disciple in the right sense of the word. In may not seem very bad to many, but there is a thin thread connecting the pupil with his spiritual guide, and at any moment this can easily break, once broken it can never be mended."

Pir Zia states at this point in the narrative that family lore has it that Inayat wished to return to India, and was only forestalled by the pleading of his family, who feared if he left Europe he would not return. Clearly needing a change of scene, he sailed for New York, intending another tour of America. He wrote to Rabia from New York,

".. After the Geneva council, if not for the cause I would have left the whole affair and gone to the East."

Prior to his departure for New York, Inayat performed an initiation and investiture of his sons Vilayat and Hidayat, age eleven and ten, as Khalifas, lieutenants in the Sufi Order. This would have important future repercussions. This event was echoed many years later when Pir Vilayat appointed his own son Zia as the future head of the Sufi Order.

America and India - The Last Days of Inayat Khan

Inayat Khan was hampered by ill health throughout the 1926 American tour. By now expert in gaining the attention of newspapers, he met such celebrities as Henry Ford, and gave several standing-room only lectures in the Detroit area. By February 1926 he was in northern California, reunited with Rabia and her groups. He met Nyogen Senzaki (1876-1958), a famous Zen teacher, through Rabia. Senzaki later published an article about their meeting titled 'Mohammedan Zen: Sufism in America.' Samuel Lewis, who claimed to have been initiated in the astral planes by Inayat Khan, was granted six interviews. Lewis later stated that in the second of these, Khan bitterly complained about how few loyal *murids* he actually could claim; if true, he was still showing disapproval of the recent Council meeting in Geneva.

Inayat returned to Europe, but clearly no healing had taken place between him and the Executive Committee. He was determined to leave for India, accompanied only by a secretary, and boarded ship from Italy on September 28, 1926. Landing in Karachi, he traveled to Lahore and then Delhi. Khan had been away from India for sixteen years. Recounted in Pir Zia's dissertation, Inayat Khan wrote his wife:

> "My impression of India is not altogether good; perhaps it is partly owing to my condition [his health] and partly by staying in Europe for so long. I have become more critical. They seem to me neglectful, dreamy..."

Inayat Khan did seek help for his physical ailments, and while in Delhi reunited with Khwaja Hasan Nizami. Nizami (1873-1955) was a prominent Chishti, keeper of the famous Dargah of Hazrat Nizamuddin Awliya, and proprietor of his own Sufi newspaper, in which he published an account of their visit, terming Khan as "our Murshid."

In January 1927, after some travels in northern India, Inayat traveled to Ajmer, Rajasthan, to attend the *urs* (death anniversary) of Khwaja Moinuddin Chishti, founder of the Order in India. Pir Zia reports, "Soon after optimistically reporting 'Coming to Ajmer has done my broken spirit good,' he was overtaken by severe influenza." Inayat returned to Delhi in mid-January and went downhill quickly, possibly from pneumonia.

He passed on at his Tilak Lodge residence in Delhi on the morning of February 5th, 1927, at age 44.

The Succession

A nineteen-page article was printed in the November 2004 issue of *Glow International*, a journal dedicated to Meher Baba. The authorship is unclear, although it begins with a page-long letter from Murshida Carol Weyland Conner, of Sufism Reoriented. In the body of the text, we are told that Inayat Khan informed his dear friend, fellow Chishti and spiritual advisor Hasan Nizami (' ... the most prominent Sufi leader of India') that he had appointed Rabia full Murshida, a fact affirmed by Nizami when he (re)appointed her a full *murshid* in Delhi in 1939:

> "Seven days before Inayat Khan's death, he (Inayat) told Hasan Nizami that he had named Rabia Martin, the American Murshida, as his successor."

Inayat Khan's attorney, Enrique Zanetti, who had revised the constitution of the Sufi Movement, invited Rabia Martin to a meeting held in Suresnes. Both Zanetti, the Executive Supervisor, and Talwar Dussaq, General Secretary of the Sufi Movement, seemed ready to accept Martin's claim as Khan's successor as the Representative General, seen as an administrative, exoteric position.

Pir Zia states:

"Dussaq's reasoning was threefold:
1. Martin was the senior Murshida
2. Martin had proven administrative ability
3. Inayat Khan had praised Martin's devotion to the Message."

Martin's internal map and perceptions proved to be quite different. Her actions and words in her only visit to the complex political infighting in the Sufi Movement headquarters appeared to be unfortunate. She seemed to misread the entire situation. She lost the support of both Zanetti and Dussaq in one event, the Sacred Readings of The Master.

She began by addressing people she barely knew, some of whom had worked for the past sixteen years to rise in the European Sufi Movement, as "..my dear *murids*." She then declined to read the prescribed Sacred Words of the Master, and declared: "I have not crossed the ocean to read to you from a paper, but to give you a solid teaching!"

She lost any chance of acceptance at that point. The International Executive Committee met at Geneva Headquarters in September of 1927. The primary issue on the table was to appoint a Representative General, which was the highest administrative post available, political head of the Order. Inayat's next-younger brother Maheboob Khan was elected unanimously "for an indefinite period of time."

Two years later, in a letter from 1929, Rabia wrote General Secretary Dussaq, challenging the recognition of Maheboob Khan as the esoteric Pir-o-Murshid of the entire Order, stating:

> "The Pir-o-Murshid in his *Esoteric rules* says, 'Pir-o-Murshid makes rules, his successor is designated by him.' This you must admit is definite. It is *not* a matter to be *voted upon.* And the spiritual reason why it cannot be voted upon is that it is a *Mystical* degree, and it is only the Pir-o-Murshid who can recognize and confirm this Mystical degree of attainment. This state of Hal, as you must know comes only by the divine favor of Allah ... In 1923 when Holy Mur-

shid came to America after an absence of eleven years, he remained as a guest in my home for more than six weeks. During that blessed and holy time he conferred an Initiation upon me as a preparation for the one he completed when he was with us again in 1926. On March 16, 1926, he conferred another, most holy Initiation, his last, and that Initiation made me his Esoteric successor. ... *Can you refer to a single Messenger whose Successor was chosen by vote?* Either we draw our authority from God or from man – it is one or the other." (italics and emphasis hers)

In her indignation, Rabia had utterly forgotten the events following the death of the Prophet Muhammad.

As powerful as that letter was, she never received an invitation to the next Executive Committee meeting, in 1930. That summer Samuel Lewis sent at least one letter to the Committee, stating that Inayat Khan had asserted to him in 1926 that Rabia was indeed his successor, and that he, Lewis, was to defend her and prevent her from defending herself. However, she could never resist getting a word in, and Lewis wrote, "...and this led to her downfall."

In 1930, before the meeting, Rabia was requested to provide some 'tangible proof' supporting her claims, so she sent them a letter termed by Dussaq as containing 'slanderous allegations.' Further, the Initiation she was given by Inayat Khan in 1926 had also been given to Maheboob Khan. Dussaq also pointed out that the norm for an appointee is to possess a 'written,' an *ijazat nama* or *khilafat nama*, a document mentioning the Order's *silsila* and the specific abilities and duties of the appointee. Martin offered instead a turban given her by Inayat Khan. Dussaq pointed out that Khan's son Vilayat had been given his father's personal turban.

The 1930 Executive Committee was fully attended, except, as usual, for Rabia Martin. Rabia's letter was read, and one of the members, Shahbaz Best, commented her language was 'forcible.' Pir Zia recounts:

"In her defense, Best stated, 'I would, however suggest that we should, as it were, exonerate her, because I understand that *one of her race* employs traditional language, and if we would understand that it is not necessarily personal, but an individual method of expression, we would be less moved by those words.' Though offered in Martin's defense, Best's identification of Martin's shortcomings as symptomatic of her Jewish identity evokes the conviction of Martin and Samuel Lewis, apparently never committed to writing but communicated orally that racism was a significant factor in the rejection of Martin's claim in Europe." (italics mine)

That 'defense' was faint praise indeed. I honor Pir Zia's honesty on the point of racism and possibly sexism. Also note that the blame does not fall on male Indian Muslim relatives-of-Inayat, protecting their sources of income, but upon the voting members of this Executive Committee, who were mostly white Europeans. He also says there is anecdotal, not written, evidence, that both Martin and Lewis believed there was anti-semitism involved in the Executive Committee's decision.

Pir Zia reproduces Dussaq's reply to Martin in full:

"This statement seems to me most extraordinary for is it not strange that Pir-o-Murshid kept all the Murshidas, yourself included, and Khalifs and Shaiks of the Sufi Order ignorant that you were to be his Successor, but made the disclosure of it to Mr. Samuel Lewis, who has no standing in the Sufi Order, for whatever be the value, in your eyes, to be a 'Khalif by spiritual degree.' However let us admit that Mr. Lewis' statement was true and that he did not misinterpret the Master's words, or that he did not imagine it, which is likely—for is it not well known that certain visionaries are subject to strange delusions and hallucinations, and you have declared, as well as Mr. Lewis himself, that he has visions—even supposing his statement to be correct, we cannot take it into consideration, for we happen to have in this office written instructions from Our Blessed Master urging us never to act upon anyone's saying, 'Murshid has told me,' but only to act upon what Murshid himself had told us."

This is an extremely interesting letter. Dussaq says Samuel Lewis had 'no standing in the Sufi Order,' and proceeds to mock Lewis for his 'visions,' even though Inayat Khan himself had said that Lewis could indeed channel him (Khan) regardless of time or space. The 'visions' comment seems to illustrate the gulf between the arid political environment of Geneva and Martin's geographically isolated Order. She had created, under Inayat Khan's direction, an Indian, traditional, spiritually-oriented group, where there was a direct link between members' ranks and their level of illumination. The reason Murshida Martin did not simply appoint Samuel Lewis as *khalifa*, or lieutenant, or why this was not recognized in Geneva, may not be recoverable.

The traditional Chishti *sama* or *qawwali* singing is designed to invoke *hal*, an ecstatic, visionary state, in the participants. General Secretary Dussaq's dry and biting wit is hardly indicative of an ecstatic experience. However, in his defense, since the 1880s, the popular press had colored and confused genuine spiritual movements with Spiritualism and Occultism, with their myriad fake mediums and apparitions. Dussaq may have heard entirely too much about 'visions.' But he did manage to completely discount and ignore the perceptions of both Martin and Lewis – Khan's apparent protégé in America, and one of Inayat's hand picked and trained *murids*.

The 1930 vote to elect Maheboob Khan as esoteric Head and Pir-o-Murshid of the Sufi Order failed, and the Committee split somewhat acrimoniously, with several European and British members severing all ties to the Sufi Movement.

When Rabia Martin received the news in San Francisco, she declared herself the Representative General of the Sufi Movement (the exoteric administrative title she claimed not to want) and announced that she 'no longer recognized the authority of Headquarters.' It seems paradoxical, to simultaneously separate from an organization and announce oneself as its head.

Failure To Communicate

What could have caused such a series of apparent missteps from someone groomed to be Inayat Khan's successor? It is clear from all accounts that Khan prized Rabia highest of all his trainees on both sides of the Atlantic.

Pir Zia's dissertation goes on for hundreds of pages, many of them describing at length the multiple Centers, the Byzantine political and organizational structures, created in Europe by Inayat Khan over time. *Cherags*, untold committees and administrative sub-sub positions, all of it held together by Khan's Rasul-like charisma.

For years on end, Murshida Rabia Martin's only connection to the Sufi work was the occasional instructional letter from Inayat Khan, now gone. She was over six thousand miles away in California, in an era where long distance international phone calls were a generation or two away, where she studied Arabic and the Qur'an and trained her own *murids* in the traditional Chishti manner, in a simple, two-layer organization. She had been busy, with Inayat Khan's emphatic approval, recreating a medieval, spiritual Sufi Order in California.

Her error in misreading the status-conscious hierarchically-oriented Europeans, and committing personal *faux pas*, led to being shut out of the succession deliberations almost completely. She only visited Europe once between 1927 and the final break in 1930, and was not present for the infighting in the many subsequent meetings to choose Khan's successor. She was the apparent victim of a political process and structure she simply did not understand and of which she was not a part.

Rabia never had a chance.

For all the voting, factions, and meetings the Europeans had, it strikes me how ethnocentric they were in the search for Khan's spiritual and temporal successor. Did it occur to no one in the Sufi Movement, especially the Indian relatives, to journey to Ajmer or Delhi and lay this at the feet of the Shaik ul Mashaik? (the world leader of the Chishti Order.) The answer lies between the lines in Pir Zia's history. The European Sufis had deified Inayat to the point where they referred to him as *Rasul*, i.e. one with, or on a level with, the Prophet Muhammad. Therefore there was no one in India, in their view, worth turning to. It's possible no one could have measured up. They may also have had the European subconscious and unspoken contempt for (brown-skinned) colonials from the Subcontinent. So their own psychology limited their search for a temporal and spiritual replacement to within their own ranks.

Thus Maheboob, the next younger brother, held the position of Representative General until Inayat's son Vilayat was old enough.

Every sign points to Martin's understanding of her role as Khan's *spiritual* successor. Note her disdain of the European group's process and especially of voting in a successor. "Either we draw our authority from God or from man – it is one or the other," she had said.

When Failure And Success Are The Same

For those who know their Muslim history, she holds a position similar to Hazrat 'Ali's in the Muslim community, which had elected - *voted for* - Abu Bakr after the death of the Prophet. The Prophet had declared, "I am the city of wisdom, and 'Ali is the door to it." 'Ali was the vessel carrying spiritual knowledge to the world. Abu Bakr was older, an established part of the Muslim community, and became the First Caliph, successor to the Prophet, because he *simply got more votes*.

To his credit, Pir Zia acknowledges the similarity of Rabia Martin's situation to the Abu Bakr - 'Ali schism (that is, the Sunni-Shia split) in the early Muslim community. This Sunni - Shia (Shiati 'Ali' means supporter of 'Ali) divide survives to the present day and is the cause of much suffering in the Muslim world.

What Pir Zia appears to have missed, or at least did not discuss, is that all Sufi orders, Sunni and Shia, except for one (Naqshbandi-Haqqani) have 'Ali right behind the Angel Jibreel (Gabriel) and the Prophet in their Silsila, the chain of succession. Fourteen hundred years of Sufis have considered Hazrat 'Ali to have had something crucial for the spiritual development of mankind, conveyed in the traditional transmission of knowledge from *murshid* to *murid*, the goal being the illumination of the student.

Pir Zia may not have wished to introduce this thought because it inevitably proceeds to the next idea: if rejected Rabia was that generation's rejected 'Ali, carrying the spiritual charge, *where does that leave the various other Sufi Order/Movement branches?*

Famed author and Sufi Idries Shah writes at length regarding what he terms 'remnant cults,' organizations which persist, sometimes for generations, long after the *baraka*, or original spiritual charge, is gone.

Epilog

This chapter described a split in the Western Sufi groups established by Hazrat Inayat Khan : the California groups led by Murshida Martin, and several Sufi Movement groups in Europe and the Americas. A major one, currently called the Inayati Order, is led at this time by Pir Zia Inayat Khan, HIK's grandson.

Murshida Martin's San Francisco and Marin County groups continued through the early 1940's, when she determined that the leading spiritual personage on the planet was Avatar Meher Baba in Maharastra State, India. She turned over the two groups to him in a letter, probably in 1945. She gave her *murids* a choice whether to stay on, with Meher Baba as the focus, rather than the Prophet Muhammad. Some portion stayed with her. Rabia Martin passed in 1947. In 1952 the charter of Sufism Reoriented was created under Meher Baba's direction.

2018

AMONG THE SLEEPING

MY STORY

The man I will refer to as Abdul Samad (slave of the Eternal) and I worked for the same Dearborn, MI automotive company starting in 1972. I was 22, a musician, a recovering hippie, deeply infected by the Beatles and the lure of the Mystic East. My reading then included Paramahansa Yogananda and A.C. Bhaktivendanta Swami Prabhuprada (founder of ISKCON) - and I recall playing *ragas* endlessly on the stereo. About the time I met Samad, I had discovered a new set of books, by G.I. Gurdjieff and acolytes like Ouspensky.

Samad was a Pakistani engineer, in the US on the equivalent of an H1B visa, going to university and working full time. He'd brought his wife and young son along. He read the Gurdjieff along with me, heavy going indeed, and we had many happy lunches in the shadow of the Ford Rouge auto plant, discussing various forms of spirituality and eating his wife's spicy goat-meat *samosas*.

Over time we moved on to Idries Shah's books, a wonderful introduction to the history and development of Islamic Sufism.

We both became interested in Chishti Hazrat Inayat Khan's and Samuel L. (Sufi Ahmad Murad) Lewis' books. Lewis' various initiations by India and Pakistani Chistis, Qadiris and Naqshbandis in his various visits to India in the early 1960's fired both our imaginations. Finding an American who had been initiated this deeply into the heart of Sufism was very exciting.

After several years of friendship, I gradually discovered Abdul Samad and his wife were longtime *murids* of a famous Chishti *murshid* in Karachi, Pakistan, Mohammed Jamil Arifi Sahib, 'Sarkar' to his followers. Sarkar had evidently been initiated into ten separate Sufi orders. I had some extraordinary dreams, and dreams are especially meaningful to Chishtis.. Abdul Samad encouraged me to write them down and send them to Sarkar. The message came through: "clean your heart."

Over the next several years Abdul Samad was able to travel back to see Sarkar multiple times. In 1976, I was honored to be a witness to Samad's naturalization ceremony: he became an American citizen. He also earned at least one doctorate in those same years, and went to work for one of the Big Three American auto companies. I spent many evenings at his house, discussing practical spirituality, Islam, and listening to Qawwali records.

In the summer of 1977, Samad and I visited Lama Foundation in northern New Mexico, where Alpert's *Be Here Now* and Pir Vilayat Khan's *Toward The One* were published, and where Samuel Lewis' *maqbara* (grave) sits in a clearing in a pine forest looking over the Rio Grande valley. At that time Abdul Samad told me he had been made Khalifa, able to start a branch of the Chishti order in the USA, should that be necessary. He had been initiated into at least four Sufi orders that I know of – Chisti, Qadiri, Naqshbandi, and Suhrawardi.

Six months later, Abdul Samad, having given me a Sufi name, instructed me to travel again to Lama, in the winter months when visitors were not allowed. I did so, and since the Lama residents remembered my visit with Abdul

Samad, they allowed me to stay at Lama for a while. I again visited Sam Lewis's grave on that mountainside and had an unusual experience; I could have found the gravesite with my eyes closed, like knowing where a hot stove is in a cold room. The snow had melted back about 20 feet in all directions. I felt privileged to experience this *baraka*. Later that day, looking out over the Rio Grande valley, there was another experience of profound gratitude and melting-of-the-heart.

Back in Detroit, I met some Sufi Order USA followers of Hazrat Inayat Khan – and later visited the Abode of the Message in New Lebanon, NY, where I met Pir Vilayat several times.

Abdul Samad does not have an active circle. He is one of the hidden ones. After a visit to Pakistan, he said he had, by his *murshid's* grace, 'graduated' to full *murshid* status.

There is an enormous mideastern population in the Detroit area, primarily in and around Dearborn. In 1979 and 1980 I studied Arabic for about 18 months. I also attended a Dearborn mosque for some time. This did not last. I was as out of place among Qur'anpounders as I'd have been among Bible-beaters. During that period Samad told me my Arabic sounded Syrian, which made sense, as my instructor was a Syrian.

However, desperate for change and more sun, I made plans to leave the Detroit area in 1982 without his permission. Also, to be perfectly honest, I hadn't honored certain tenets according to instructions.

About that time, Sarkar passed away. The story Samad told me was that Sarkar was sitting in circle with his followers. He leaned over and whispered to his eldest son, "...time for a change of weather," and died instantly.

There in Detroit Samad told me that since I wasn't following the rules I could not play the game, that I should no longer consider myself affiliated with the Chishti-Qadiri orders, and that I should not ask for help from Sam Lewis or Inayat Khan. He did challenge me to find the local spiritual chargeman for the area where I would settle. I took that instruction quite seriously.

My travels took me around the USA, where I reconnected with my future wife and settled in Arizona where she joined me and we were married. For 14 years I had no contact with Abdul Samad. He called me in 1996 and invited me to travel with him to Ajmer, India, home of Khwaja Moinuddin Chishti's tomb-shrine, or dargah. This invitation led me to believe I had in fact cleaned my heart sufficiently to pass muster with the Sufis. However, I declined the invitation, choosing instead to invest six months in a disastrous venture into the film business, where I crashed on a Harley, coming back home with a smashed knee, on crutches and oxygen.

In 2001 Abdul Samad wrote me again, inviting me to India. I again declined, not wanting to be a hypocrite and pretend to be a dutiful Muslim Sufi. Heading off to Ajmer alone, Abdul Samad subsequently wrote me a series of God intoxicated letters in which he referred to me by the Sufi name he had bestowed on me years before. Over the next couple of years, he kindly made substantial suggestions and revisions to this article on Sufism via email.

In 2006 Abdul Samad's daughter came through my town, and she had dinner with my wife and myself at our home. She called me Uncle Karl, which makes sense, in that her father is my dear brother. The next year, spring of 2007, I traveled back to Michigan in order to bury my father's ashes in the family plot. Now retired, Abdul Samad invited me to his home twice for dinner. He showed me Sarkar's picture for the first time, indicated he was in regular contact with Sarkar (remember Sufis consider that the adept may be contacted regardless of time or space) and discussed his last visit to Ajmer. He now stays with Moinuddin Chishti's own descendants, keepers of the famous Dargah, when he is in Ajmer, at the heart of the Chishti Order. He told me some amazing stories of staying up all night in the courtyard outside Khwaja's tomb.

In 2010 I was honored to lead the *zikr* of over twenty fellow pilgrimswhile at the Dargah of Hazrat Moinuddin Chishti in Ajmer, Rajasthan, India. Our party included an elderly man, Don E. Stevens, the only surviving *murid* of Murshida Rabia Martin, Hazrat Inayat Khan's first Western disciple.

There has been sporadic email correspondence with Abdul Samad in the past five years. He is now widowed and his children have moved away.

Arabic/Persian Glossary

Al-Asr – afternoon prayer
Al-Razzaq - 'the Sustainer'. One of Islam's 99 names of God.
Adab – manners, comportment.
Ahwal – inner states.
Al-Khidr – the Green Saint. An immortal servant of Allah.
Allah - the creator, the highest being. God.
Allahu Akbar – God is most great
Arif – the knower, the wise.
Awliya – saints.
Baqa - subsistence in Oneness with God.
Baraka – a byproduct of Sufi 'work'. Power or blessing.
Bida'a – unwelcome innovation since the time of the Prophet.
Caliph – successor to the Prophet Muhammad. The first 4 Caliphs were Abu Bakr, Umar, Uthman, and Ali.
Dervish – a Sufi. Mainly refers to members of the Mevlevi Order.
Dhikr - literally, 'remembrance' of Allah. Phrases used by Sufis.
Du'a – specific pose and prayer.

Fana – literally, 'annihalation', re: to the Nafs, or personal ego.
Fana fi Murshid – absorption into one's teacher.
Fana fi Rasul – absorption into the Prophet Muhammad.
Fana fi Shaikh – absorption into the founder of the Order.
Fana fillah, Fana fi-Allah – absorption into the Creator.
Faqih – an Islamic jurist.
Fard - a spiritually advanced Muslim with no Sufi history.
Fatwa – clarifying opinions of Islamic jurists on specific cases.
Fiqh – the 'understanding' or opinions of Islamic jurists.
Firasat – intuitive insight, relating to Murshid – Murid relations.
Ghaus – helper, or helper of Allah.
Ghaus, Ghous – a condition where the body may fall to pieces during Zikr or while sleeping. Rare.
Ghaus-I-Azam - 'the greatest Ghaus'. Hazrat Abdal Qadir Gilani.
Habs-i-dam - restraint of breath. (dam is 'breath' in Persian.) Naqsh.

Hadith – the authenticated words of the Prophet.
Hafiz – one who has memorized the Qur'an. Also, a famous Sufi poet.
Hajj – the obligatory pilgrimage to Mecca.
Hal – a 'state' of ecstacy in a Sama gathering.
Halal – permitted, approved.
Haqq, Haqiqa – Truth, Reality. State of realization of Allah.
Haram – forbidden, unlawful.
Hazrat – the 'Presence'. One in whom the presence of God is felt.
Hijira – the Prophet's retreat from a hostile Mecca to a welcoming Medina in 579AD. Year 1 in the Islamic calendar.
Ijaza Nama – the document of investiture given to an accredited Murshid in an established Sufi Order.
Ilm al-Huduri – 'knowledge by presence', a distance teaching technique of the Shia Sufis. (Isfahan School, Suhrawardiyya)
Insani Kamil – the complete man. The Prophet. A perfected being.
Islam - surrender.
Isnad – the chain of attribution for each Hadith.
Istafar'Allah - forgive me God.
Jadhba – divine Love.

Jamal – beauty.
Jamali – a dervish of modest demeanor and mild temperament.
Jelal – majesty.
Jelalli – a dervish of fiery and intense temperament.
Jibreel – the angel Gabriel.
Kaaba – Abraham's house in Mecca.
Kaffir – an unbeliever.
Kalimah – the Muslim testimony of faith: "Ashhadu an la ilaha illa Allah wa Muhammad ar-Rasul Allah": "I believe there is no deity but Allah and Muhammad is his Messenger."
Kamil Shaikh – the perfected Sufi teacher.
Karamat – a major miracle.
Khalif, Khalifa – an assistant to a Murshid.
Kharabat – the Sufi poet's 'Tavern of Ruin'.
Khirqa – the Sufi robe of initiation given to Khalifas or Murshids.
Khwaja – 'master'.
Khwajagan – the 'masters'. The original name of the Naqshbandi Order.
Madhabs – schools of Islamic jurisprudence. There are four in the Sunni world, and they resemble one another closely.
Mahdzub (Arabic), mast (Hindi) – one absorbed in the inner planes.

Malamati – the 'blameworthy' approach to mysticism.
Maqam, Maqqamat – stations on the Sufi path.
Mashhur – 'well known'. An acknowledged teacher with a following.
Mastur – secret, or hidden. A Sufi whose work does not include training murids.
Maya – the illusory reality. (Hindu)
Murid – an aspirant or student of the Sufi Way.
Murshid – an accredited teacher in the Sufi Way.
Murshida – a female teacher.
Mutashabbihun – people who try to resemble Sufis. (Suhrawardi)
Mutawassit – a Sufi of middle rank.
Nafs – the false self, the ego. That which separates us from Allah.
Nur-I-Muhammad – the 'light' of Muhammad.
Pir – an accredited teacher of the Sufi Way. Literally, 'elder'.
Qalandar – a wandering, impolite dervish.
Qalb – the human heart (Ar.)
Qawwali – music used in Chishti 'sama' sessions. Qawwal – musician.
Qur'an – the book dictated to the Prophet by the Angel Gabriel over many years. The Word of Allah.

Qutb – a spiritual 'pillar', center of mystic activity.
Rab'ta – heart-to-heart bonding between Sufis.
Rajab – a month in the Islamic calendar
Rakat – prostration in prayer, or Salat.
Ramadhan – prescribed annual fast.
Rasul – messenger (of Allah) referring to the Prophet Muhammad.
Salat – prayer, 5 times daily.
Sama – 'audition'. Sufi meetings where music and Zikr are utilized.
Shaikh, Shaykh – an accredited teacher in the Sufi Way. Pl. 'Shuyuk'.
Sharia – Islamic law : Qur'an, Hadith, Sunna, Fatwas, Fiqh.
Shia, Shi'ite, Shi'ati Ali – the body of Muslims who believe Caliph Ali was the Prophet's rightful successor.
Shirk – a major sin, placing anyone or anything on a level with Allah.
Silsila – 'chain' of personal spiritual transmission in a Sufi order, beginning with the Prophet, the angel Gabriel/Jibreel.
Suhba – a teacher's speech at a gathering.
Sunna – the body of words and actions of the Prophet Muhammad.

Sunni – the body of Muslims who believe Abu Bakr, the first Caliph, was the rightful successor to the Prophet. Following the Sunna.
Sura – a chapter or section of the Qur'an.
Tariqa – an order or 'way' in Sufism. Pl. 'Turuq'.
Tasnim – water well in heaven
Tassawur-I-Shaikh – 'blending' with the Shaikh, at a distance.
Tauhid, Tawheed – the monotheist concept There Is No Deity But Allah, 'La ilaha illa Allah.'
Tawaj – direct transmission of wisdom. (Naqshbandi)
Ulema – a collection of Faqih, or Islamic Jurists.
Waliullah – 'friend of Allah'. Enlightened Sufi or mystic.
Wazifa – silently repeated Zikr. Naqshbandi.
Zakat – a percentage of one's income given to charity.
Zikr – literally, 'remembrance' of Allah. Names of Allah or other phrases used by Sufis.
Ziyarat – visiting the tomb of a saint.

Among the Sleeping

Bibliography/References

"Unseen Rain" Quatrains of Rumi - Moyne/ Barks Threshold Books 1986

" Dr. Javad Nurbaksh "In The Tavern Of Ruin, Seven Essays on Sufism, pub. 1978. Italics in the original. p.107

Suhrawardi's 'Kitab Adab al-Muridin' ('A Sufi Rule For Novices') translated by Menahem Milson, Harvard University Press 1975

Muhammad el-Ghazzali, 'Ihya Ulum-id-Din,' Vol.4, p.238

Chishti Order site in Ajmer India
www.sufiajmer.com, specifcally
www.sufiajmer.org/html/khwaja_moinuddin.html

Massud Farzan, "The Tale Of The Reed Pipe", Dutton 1974

www.windsofchange.net/archives/2002_07_21_woc.html
www.gurdjieff-legacy.org/40articles/neosufism.htm

O. M. Burke, "Among the Dervishes", Dutton 1975

Seyyed Hossein Nasr, "Sufi Essays", Schocken Books 1977

www.serendipity.li/more/lessing_shah.htm - Doris Lessing on Idries Shah's works

www.clubofrome.org - Club Of Rome website
www.ishk.net - Institute for the Study of Human Knowledge

www.uga.edu/islam/sufismwest.html – listing of Western Islamic and non-Islamic Sufi organizations

www.uga.edu/islam/Sufism.html - listing of Eastern Orders and famous Sufis

Hadiths found in Sahih al-Bukhari, one of the trusted Hadith sources

J. Spencer Trimingham, "The Sufi Orders in Islam", Oxford University Press, 1973

H. Talat Halman, "Where The Two Seas Meet," Fons Vitae, 2013

http://wahiduddin.net/sufi_poetry.htm - Excellent site with examples of classic poets

www.sufistudies.net/world-community/shabistari.html - Analysis of Shabistari and Rumi

The Holy Qur'an, translated by Marmaduke Pickthall, Sh. M. Ashraf, Lahore, Pakistan

Dr. Javad Nurbakhsh, "Sufi Symbolism" vol. 1 Khaniqahi Nimatullahi Publications

Hakim Sanai, 'The Walled Garden of the Truth'/ The Hadiqa of Hakim Sanai, translated 1908 by Major J. Stephenson, pub. Samuel Weiser, 1972

http://www.themodernreligion.com/basic/madhab/madhab-nec.htm
http://groups.yahoo.com/group/sufis_without_borders/message/13158

http://books.guardian.co.uk/print/0,3858,5326079-99931,00.html Turkish Sufism http://www.sabiree.com/sufism/sama_book/role_of_sama.htm Chishti Sama

http://www.almusaffir.com/modules/myalbum Qawwali music

PLEASE NOTE: Internet websites are ephemeral in nature. Not all of these pages will be available in perpetuity. However, there is a wonderful website which maintains earlier versions of thousands of websites:

www.archive.org

* * *

786

Ishq Allah maa'bud Lillah

AMBKJ
* * *

Among the Sleeping

www.ingramcontent.com/pod-product-compliance
Lightning Source LLC
Chambersburg PA
CBHW031416290426
44110CB00011B/411